The Experience of Nothingness

The Experience of Nothingness

MICHAEL NOVAK

HARPER COLOPHON BOOKS

Harper & Row, Publishers

New York, Evanston, San Francisco, London

For Karen, Richard, and Tanya
—Experience of Everything

The Experience of Nothingness. Copyright ©1970 by Michael Novak. All rights reserved. Printed in the United States of America. No part of this book may be used or reproduced in any manner whatsoever without written permission except in the case of brief quotations embodied in critical articles and reviews. For information address Harper & Row, Publishers, Inc., 49 East 33rd Street, New York, N.Y. 10016. Published simultaneously in Canada by Fitzhenry & Whiteside Limited, Toronto.

First HARPER COLOPHON Edition published 1971

Standard Book Number: 06-090239-6

Contents

Acknowledgments

The author is grateful to the following sources for the use of published materials:

American Academy of Arts and Letters for *Daedalus: Symbolism in Religion and Literature*.

The Estate of Henry James for the letter from William James.

The Free Press for *World Politics and Personal Insecurity* by Harold Lasswell.

Harvard University Press, The Loeb Classical Library, for *Aristotle: The Nicomachean Ethics* (H. Rackham, trans.).

John Hopkins Press for *Mind: An Essay on Human Feelings* by Suzanne Langer.

Little, Brown & Co. for *The Thought and Character of William James* by Ralph Barton Perry.

McGraw-Hill Book Company for *Soul on Ice* by Eldridge Cleaver.

David McKay Company, Inc. for *The Varieties of Religious Experience* by William James.

Newman Press for *The Ascent of Mount Carmel* by St. John of the Cross (E. A. Peers, trans.).

W. W. Norton & Company, Inc. for *Identity: Youth and Crisis* and *Insight and Responsibility* by Erik Erikson.

Pantheon Books, Inc. for *The Politics of Experience* by R. D. Laing and *Madness and Civilization* by Michel Foucault.

Random House for *The Stranger* by Albert Camus; *Culture Against Man* by Jules Henry; *The Will to Power* by Friedrich Nietzsche (Walter Kaufmann, trans.).

University of Illlinois Press for *The Symbolic Uses of Politics* by Murray Edelman.

Preface to the Colophon Edition

The response to the hardcover edition of this book taught me two things. First, older readers seem to have broken through the American "system of meaning" more thoroughly than younger readers. Many of the young still seem to be tempted by traditional American illusions—that the annunciation of moral goals is itself a moral act, that moral energy is the same as or better than political energy, that "progress" will come more or less automatically from good will (or other changes in consciousness), that morality consists in the individual's "doing his thing" (hoary *laissez faire*), that there lurks up ahead somewhere, behind a hidden door, under a tree, within some hidden cave, a greening light of hope and prosperity and bliss: some magical dream drawing all Americans onward.

Many Americans, old and young, have seen too much, and absorbed too much pain to go on believing in mirages. Life is much more terrifying than easy hope pretends. Ugly, boring, painful, vastly disillusioning experiences stalk our lives. There is much more solitude in life than anything in the ideology of our education teaches us. The gratifications and excitements of upward mobility sooner or later abandon us to the dizzying inner spaces of our rootlessness.

To be sure, many Americans desire to cover over inner terror, to shrug it off as momentary weariness, to brighten and to smile and to look for something "constructive" to do. Many keep faith. But others grow.

The generation that went to college in the fifties, my own generation, was preparing itself for the long haul. We were somewhat "silent." But also serious. The young who followed us, in the sixties, burnt their candles at both ends, in spectacular light. Each generation has its own strength, and weakness. Ours knows well the experience of nothingness, the contours of compromise and illusion, the masks of security. If we no longer seem to hope—do not believe it is from weakness; it is from strength. Facile and illusory American hope has no power over us. Our hope is an acceptance of despair.

The second insight critical reaction brought to me is that many do not take seriously enough the *nothingness* of the experience of nothingness. Many who enter into the experience never emerge again. Insanity, pretense, mere conventionality, no-think, suicide, cynicism, egocentrism, a wild drug-taking race toward an early death, an intense desire to be consumed like flame—have we not seen in the last decade countless forms of self-destruction in the name of inner emptiness? It is not by chance that films like *Bonnie and Clyde, Easy Rider, Butch Cassidy and the Sundance Kid,* and even *Joe* end in orgies of blood and death. It is not by chance that so many cultural heroes end up dead with needle-pointed arms in chill hotel rooms far from their homes. Listen to the wild beat of rock: hear the intensity of death.

I am far from trying to show that our nothingness is unreal, further still from pulling a rabbit of hope out of a hat. Let those who wish to commit suicide commit suicide: I lay no imperative upon anyone. What has caught my eye in the history of nihilism is that Nietzsche, Sartre, and others *wrote books:* a most committed and disciplined use of time. The same drive that led them to the experience of nothingness seemed to teach them other values as well—and without contradiction. Today, in any case, the experience of nothingness is simply a fact: many of us have it. What did we have to do to get it? It arises only under certain conditions. What are these conditions?

The form of the question as it arises today is: *Granted that I have the experience of nothingness, what shall I do with it?*

Perhaps nothing at all. Perhaps kill myself, go mad, look for a cause, turn on the radio, look for someone to hug, lie down and fall into an endless sleep, become a sleepwalker, drift, pretend . . . The possibilities are limitless.

To my knowledge, no one who has reflected upon the experience of nothingness has called attention to the unique moral conditions under which it appears. These conditions do not disappear when the experience of nothingness seeps like fog into one's consciousness. There is no obligation to notice what these conditions are. There is no obligation, once noticing them, to reinforce them and to build one's life upon them. That is only one choice among many. That is merely something we *can* do, if we wish, without falsifying the experience of nothingness in the least.

This book, then, is at most an invitation. *Notice,* it says, *everything you can about what is happening to you. Do not avert your eyes from the commitments which are in fact, if you experience nothingness, already operating in you.* You need not do either of these things. But you may. If you do, you "structure" the experience of nothingness—by calling operations within yourself into consciousness, which you might otherwise not have noticed. So doing, you do not falsify the experience, do not cancel it, do not escape from it. It becomes a source of further actions, actions which are by so much without illusion. ("By so much." Are men every wholly without illusion? No.)

From year to year, the experience of nothingness grows deeper in one's life, takes a more inclusive and profounder hold. By no means is this book intended to remove, cover over, or alleviate that experience. I want to unmask one piece of ideology only—that the experience of nothingness necessarily incapacitates one from further action.

Every form placed upon the experience of nothingness is ideological, including the form suggested here. The one advantage I claim for the course I have followed is that it keeps open the cellar doors; the cool draughts of the experience of nothingness remain one's constant companion, one's constant critic, one's constant stimulus. *If you desire to possess everything, desire to have nothing.*

Finally, the reflections on political action in Chapter IV are not meant to heap contempt on democratic forms of political life. They are intended to point out the void whence these forms spring, which they do not cover. Democracy is an illusory form of government. Although among illusions it is the least murderous, its hands too know blood, dry and caked, freshly red. We work as in a darkness—work, and yet do not wish to be deceived. If everything is meaningless, we come to such perception only through a most scrupulous fidelity, an honorable fraternity. If these too are meaningless, they remain one disposition open to us. They invite, they do not compel. Granted that we have the experience of nothingness, what shall we do with it?

January, 1971   MICHAEL NOVAK

Note

This brief philosophical essay was first prepared for delivery as the four Bross Lectures at Lake Forest College in January 1969. I am grateful to President William Graham Cole, Dean William Dunn, Professor Forest W. Hansen, and members of the community at Lake Forest for having invited me and for having responded to my work with generosity and warmth. To Dean Dunn, who arranged everything, I owe special thanks.

Kathy Mulherin offered invaluable research assistance, household confusion, and entertainment to our children. Sharon Winklhofer and Terry Linnemeyer typed, and typed, and typed.

Prologue

This philosophical voyage may be construed as a meditation on the following poem:

> *On a dark night, Kindled in love with yearnings—*
> *oh, happy chance!—*
> *I went forth without being observed, My house being*
> *now at rest.*
> *In darkness and secure, By the secret ladder, disguised*
> *—oh, happy chance!*
> *In darkness and in concealment, My house being*
> *now at rest.*
> *In the happy night, In secret, when none saw me,*
> *Nor I beheld aught, Without light or guide, save that*
> *which burned in my heart.*
> *This light guided me More surely than the light of*
> *noonday,*
> *To the place where he (well I knew who!) was awaiting*
> *me—*
> *A place where none appeared.*

St. John of the Cross
"Prologue," *Ascent of Mount Carmel*

1

The Experience of Nothingness

The experience of nothingness is an incomparably fruitful starting place for ethical inquiry. It is a vaccine against the lies upon which every civilization, American civilization in particular, is built. It exposes man as animal, question-asker, symbol-maker.

I wish to show from the experience of nothingness that no man *has* a self or an identity; in a society like ours he must constantly be *inventing* selves. I also wish to show that even the most solid and powerful social institutions, though they may imprison us, impoverish us, or kill us, are fundamentally mythical structures designed to hold chaos and formlessness at bay: they are more like dreams than like reality. The experience of nothingness, with or without psychoanalytic, social, and theological criticism, dissolves the pragmatic solidity of the American way of life.

The hopes of those young people who desire to bring about a revolution in America seem doomed to bitter and painful frustration; the experience of nothingness, carefully reflected upon, might arm them against that event. I hope to write of that experience in a way that leads not to passivity or to a sense of defeat, but to calm ardor and revolutionary expectation.[1]

1. The Pursuit of Happiness

In American society the pursuit of happiness has almost attained the status of a constitutional right. Yet is it wise, or human, or good to pursue happiness? At any cost? At anyone's expense? By any deeds whatever? A small number of men and women have no special right, have they, to accept a major part of the wealth of the entire planet? May they pursue their own happiness with little regard for the lot of the vast majority of men?

Americans think of happiness as a psychological state of contentment or fulfillment, in which pleasure outbalances pain.[2] Yet the psychological states of essentially white, middle class Americans may not be so sacred that all other values, purposes, and meanings in the universe must be subservient to them. Many Americans imagine that the conditions of happiness can be satisfied by a balanced diet, suburban living, social status, and success in one's marriage and work. If a college coed writes home to her mother that she is restless and ill at ease, her mother is not likely to write back: "Don't worry, darling, it's only the ontological anxiety that all of us must share." She will more likely write: "Are you sure you're eating well? Are you getting enough sleep?" One would think, to watch the frequency with which Americans smile and assure each other that they are happy, that it is unpatriotic for an American to be discontent. "AMERICA: LOVE IT OR LEAVE IT!" the bumper stickers say.

From 1870 to 1940, the experience of nothingness swept through the educated class of Europe. The "disease" hardly seemed to touch well-fed, active, busy Americans. Even philosophers like Sidney Hook[3] and Charles Frankel[4] found existentialist literature on the subject vague, foreign, and self-serving. In America things were always looking up.

It seems indispensable to a technological society like ours to be future-oriented, forward-looking, fascinated by hope. The illusion of progress is the prop that takes the place of God; many cling to it. Could Americans endure life without ever new frontiers? Our national psyche is ill at ease wherever progress, our most important product, is not evident. Our image of world history places Washington (why not Peking—older, more various, more populous, more deeply cultured?) at the cutting edge of the line of progress that passes from ancient Israel to Athens to Rome to Paris and to London. Other nations are called developed or underdeveloped by comparison with us. In American eyes the march of time is linear; its direction, despite temporary setbacks, is up.

Suppose the American myth of progress, pragmatism, and fulfillment is wrong. Suppose history is going—precisely nowhere. Suppose the human costs of progress, for which we now have no measure, are steeper than the technical gains we are so fond of measuring.[5] By assuming a new way of looking at the world, a great many young Americans have begun to disabuse themselves of the myths of the American way of life. Their precious years have sunk deep into the mud of Vietnam until they choke for breath. Ours is, they say with horror, a militarist, counterrevolutionary, racist nation.[6] For several years now, some young people have pinned their hopes upon the possibility of a revolution in American values. Many grow discouraged, disillusioned, sad. They can't go home to the suburban way of life they fled with abhorrence; the ledge ahead seems impassable. They are suspended, unable to talk with those five years older than they, some perhaps unable to talk with those five years younger.

I want to set a question before them: Have not you, too, sometimes tried with your theater of the streets, your frantic politics, to escape the feeling of nothingness? Have not you, too, like your parents, frequently turned to action as if it were a potion of forgetfulness? Are you not true children of your parents, clinging to the belief in essential human goodness, in love with quick solutions, dreaming of a gentle paradise? . . . Can action based upon evasion fail to end in bitterness?

3

2. The Experience of America

"The experience of nothingness" is an experience, not a concept. It can be pointed to, described, built up indirectly, but not defined. Meursault's experience in *The Stranger*, Tolstoy's *The Death of Ivan Illich*, Kafka's "Metamorphosis," Sartre's *The Age of Reason*, and Saul Bellow's *The Dangling Man* are among its literary expressions. The experience of nothingness, however, arises in original forms today. The literature of preceding generations comforts us that we are not alone, but it does not precisely define our state of soul.

Today, for the young, consciousness is shaped by the fluidity of percepts.[7] Undifferentiated time is the medium of consciousness, like a sea on which and in which images float. The shaper of an alert, intelligent consciousness is no longer a corpus of writings ("literature") nor the pursuit of a rigorous, analytical line of argument ("the sciences"). Many good students, of good will, who really want to read and to learn about the past, find it very difficult to concentrate. The new shaper of alert, discerning consciousness is the camera. The images on a screen are not sequential; time is dissolved, turned upon itself, defeated. The present gains at the expense of past and future. The attention of the camera zooms in, pulls back, superimposes, cuts away suddenly, races, slows, flashes back, flicks ahead, juxtaposes, repeats, spins. A turn of the wrist at the channel indicator alters reality. For those introduced to consciousness by such a teacher, the world is fluid. The percepts are too many and too rich to order, except by certain rhythms of emotion.

Roland Barthes describes in *Writing Degree Zero* the gradual collapse after 1850 of the canonical "literature" of the European aristocracy and bourgeoisie.[8] The language of the poor, the prostitutes, and the beggars entered the consciousness of writers; the pretensions of the classical and bourgeois traditions to universality were shattered. The use by middle class historians and novelists of the narrative past tense ("The marchioness went out at five

4

o'clock") and of the third person ("he") had masked an ordered worldview, a definiteness, a position in the cosmos, safely observed. Such a universe could easily be shaped by stories: beginning, middle, end. Madness, chaos, and profound diversity were neatly kept outside. After the revolution of 1848, the writer began to feel uneasy in the literary tradition; that tidy image had been shattered. He listened for a voice of his own, listened, finally, for the neutral, clear, amoral voice achieved most flawlessly by Camus in *The Stranger*. Writing moved outside "Literature," "Tradition," "Society." The human race lacks unity; the writer recognized the absence of a language of unity. He continues today to trace his personal mythic history, defeated even by his own successes: he renders his isolation only to find it debased as common currency.

But the dispersal of consciousness experienced by the younger generation in the United States goes further still. In the classic French myth, the center of consciousness is a clear eye, focusing on "clear, distinct ideas." "I *think*, therefore I am." Hence the painful clarity of French sensibility and consciousness. In the United States, in an ever growing sub-culture at least, the equivalent affirmation is simply: "I feel." No "therefore" is available, or needed. The eye of consciousness yields to affect, percept, kaleidoscope. The self is a recipient of stimuli in a darkened room. I know I am alive when a warm body is next to mine. Connections come through skin.

In the new civilization then, the primary sense of reality is shaped partly by parents and neighbors (local customs, raised eyebrows), partly by books ("the liberal tradition"), but mostly by cinema, television, and records. It is a civilization of massive dissolution.

Those whose sense of the meaningful, the relevant, and the real is not entirely shaped by the new media may feel themselves caught between two barbarisms. If they imagine the self to be a seeing eye, a fierce and mastering awareness —Reason—then they stand accused of the barbaric rationalization of human life that has yielded

5

Dallas, airline terminals, body count, and painful inner emptiness. If they imagine the self to be a center of feeling, they will certainly be drawn to darkness, blood and destruction. (The "gentle revolution" is innocent when no threat faces it. The young have learned to cope when they are shown approval. Denied their will, their aspect is terrifying. Events, inevitably harsh, will surely make them bitter; filled with resentment, distrustful, they will feel trapped, a thousand times betrayed.) Apollo sheered from Dionysus yields two tribes of beasts.

The experience of nothingness in America, however, cuts across all networks: neighbor culture, book culture, electronic culture. In every part of America the sense of security has been undermined; nearly everything must be defended. All the more because the Republic was established to ensure our happiness, we find reality too much to bear. The experience of nothingness seeps into our awareness through a sieve.

Boredom is the first taste of nothingness. Today, boredom is the chief starting place of metaphysics. For boredom leads instantly to "killing time." And why is time a threat? Time, on the stage of consciousness, stands still. For the bored, no action is more attractive than any other. The self cannot be drawn into action; it lives by and for distractions; it waits. The world acts; the self is acted on. The fighter pilot whose skeleton is supported by the web straps of a plane crashed long ago in the jungles of Iwo Jima might today be supported by the web strap of a commuter train. Death seems continuous with death-in-life. Many have an overpowering urge to sleep. When Superman meets the social worker (Jules Feiffer), he learns that he is not an agent; he is acted on, his behavior has been determined. He loses strength. He droops.

Boredom: the discovery that everything is a game. A friend of mine decided that, short of suicide, one bulwark against time is a game sufficiently complicated to hold his attention until death. He made enough money as an electronics engineer (a specialist in game theory) to have free at least one year in every three. He determined to visit every town on the planet with a population over twenty-five thousand. During his working years he pored over maps; during his traveling years he concentrated on one continent after another. He often stayed in a town only long enough to lunch and to make a mark on his list. The beauty of it is, he told me, that a booming population, wars, and refugees guarantee an ever changing list.

Besides boredom, there is the collapse of a strongly inculcated set of values. I have heard students say with bitterness that high school is "enough betrayal for a lifetime." A seeing-eye God who turns out to be on the side of parents, society, philistinism, law and order, mind and dessication. But after that, what? Many search for a new social order, a new community of love. Without a vision they would perish; a utopia becomes their crutch, filling the psychological need once filled by God. Social scientists leap in to tell the adolescent that everything is relative, that everything is determined, and to suggest that the social system is the source of his inner emptiness. (The "system" plays, today, the role of devil.) Plato: the system is the self writ large; the alienation of the self comes from the system. The young are left with the inner helplessness they learned in grammar school. Their rage is legitimated; it is projected outward. They flail against "the dehumanization of the American way of life." Although the new imperative is "Humanize the system," it is impossible to discern the criteria for "humanization." No society in history ever met all the needs the young feel. Slowly the young learn that even warm, close lovers betray one another, and each discovers in himself countless self-betrayals. Gone are the old firm values; gone also the innocent world that replaced them. Alienation projected onto the system is evasion. It evades a more terrifying emptiness.

Thirdly, there is helplessness. It is not only the large, impersonal bureaucracy that engenders feelings of helplessness. It is not only the feeling that "I have no control over my life." It is also the recognition that those who wield power are also empty, and that I, too, if I had power over my life, am most confused about what I

7

would do with it. The sense of helplessness today is not, in the end, political; power, even pressed down and running over, does not fill the void; it merely masks it. In the eyes of the successful leaders of the Students for a Democratic Society, as in those of the occupants of the White House, one may still see nothingness.

Fourthly, there is the betrayal by permissiveness, pragmatism, and value-neutral discourse. "To every child a childhood." The young have a right to learn a way of discriminating right from wrong, the posed from the authentic, the excellent from the mediocre, the brilliant from the philistine, the shoddy from the workmanlike. When no one with experience bothers to insist—to insist —on such discrimination, they rightly get the idea that discernment is not important, that no one cares, that no one cares either about such things—or about them. For it is demanding to teach children ethics, beauty, excellence; demanding in itself, and even more demanding to do so with authenticity. The laissez-faire attitude of American society in matters of the human spirit represents one of the greatest mass betrayals of responsibility by any civilization in human history. (Ironically, the young in their rebellion often manifest in the form of "Do your own thing" precisely this profound sickness of their elders.)

Fifthly, there are drug experiences, and uncounted experiences with intimacy unwanted but given anyway. The young are forced to live through the problems of technological consciousness, problems created by generations who built a rational, efficient society without calculating in advance its effect upon human beings. The apocalypse may come, not by fire or flood, but by mass insanity. The civilization in and around New York City surely manifests insanity's advancing stages: everywhere there is hostility, bitterness, resentment—that grinding, bitter resentment of which Nietzsche and Scheler warned. People lash out at one another. Parents ridicule children. Wives scream at husbands.

Everywhere there is the experience of mechanical relationships. Has anyone ever counted how many persons in the United States are paid for telling lies? Has anyone ever counted the proportion of human transactions in which Americans are forced to treat one another impersonally, superficially, without interest? It is quite plain that Americans, the most nomadic people since the medieval Arabs, seldom grow organically into marriage. When they marry, they know only a small segment—hardly the least decisive—of their partners' lives. After they marry, the lives of husbands and wives are commonly attracted into separate orbits, sheering apart from one another. Nothing organic, nothing mutually rooted.

The enormous weight, meanwhile, put upon mutual sexual fulfillment is insupportable; intercourse is an organic expression of entire psyches, not a mechanical plugging in. Among young people, the weakening of cultural forms supporting sexual rituals and restraints deprives sexual intercourse of sustenance for the imagination and the spirit. It comes too cheaply: its intimacy is mainly fake; its symbolic power is reduced to the huddling warmth of kittens in the darkness—not to be despised, but open as a raw wound to the experience of nothingness. Close your eyes and plummet through the empty space where a lover ought to be.

A complete phenomenology of the experience of nothingness in our generation is neither possible nor desirable. There are as many ways for that unmistakable experience to break into one's consciousness as there are personal histories. Some feel its touch by way of sickness or disaster, some by way of external event and others by inner breakdown, some in the flush of power and others in irretrievable despair. The experience of nothingness comes uninvited; it may also be pursued. It is not found at the boundaries of life merely, at the broken places;[9] it comes also from the very center, from the core of joy and pride and dignity. The strong nod at its voice with familiarity no less than the weak. The men and women from the lower middle class lack fancy words for it, but behind the skin of their faces it sits with the same mask it wears under the faces of television commentators.

Nor is the experience of nothingness accurately named *Angst*

9

(Kierkegaard, Heidegger). Somehow the European hungers to possess his own being, to be the cause of his own existence, to be God.[10] When he discovers that his own being is partial and invaded by nonbeing, he feels an icy threat. But the experience of nothingness in America is more often a peculiar and quiet vulnerability, a dead stillness at the center of activity, a lack of drive, an ignorance of Being and Life and Faith, a bafflement that a future that should have been so lovely turns out so bleak. The American experience of nothingness is a certain sadness. We do not have, despite our reputation, the European willfulness; behind our frenetic activity and self-assurance lurks a soft, purring, wounded kitten. We are not metaphysical but sentimental.

3. In Europe: Nihilism

One cannot, however, give the American experience voice without turning to its European background. European thinkers, of course, immediately turned the experience of nothingness, which began to "infect" Europeans with increasing frequency in the nineteenth century, into an "ism"; they spoke of it ideologically, as nihilism. They wrote from a history of unsurpassed intellectual energy. They had seen mythology, religion, and science express themselves in a brilliant sunrise of cultural history, each stage "higher" than the preceding; and then in the nineteenth century as they were stepping toward the peak of their achievement, on the threshold of a golden age, during nearly a century of relative world peace, they peered down into a fathomless abyss. Friedrich Nietzsche, like a tongue darting into a cavity, could not divert his attention. He asked himself again and again: "What does nihilism mean?" In a single felicitous sentence he answered: "The aim is lacking; 'why?' finds no answer."[11]

The experience of nothingness is a mode of human consciousness; it occurs in human beings, not in cats or trees.[12] It is, often, a kind of exhaustion of spirit that comes from seeking "meaning" too long and too ardently. It is accompanied by terror. It seems like a kind of death, an inertness, a paralysis. Meanwhile, the dark impulses of destruction find only thin resistance, they beat upon the doors for instantaneous release. The threshold of rage, suicide, and murder is frighteningly low. (Does death make any difference?) Yet even more vivid than the dark emotions are a desert-like emptiness, a malaise, an illness of the spirit and the stomach. One sees all too starkly the fraudulence of human arrangements. Every engagement seems so involved in half-truth, lie, and unimportance that the will to believe and the will to act collapse like ash.

Nietzsche distinguished three phases in the experience of nothingness, and it may be helpful to follow his notes on the subject, which are too long to quote in full.[13] "Nihilism," he wrote, "will have to be reached, *first*, when we have sought in all events a 'meaning' that is not there." Nihilism, then, is a "recognition of the long *waste* of strength"; one is "ashamed in front of oneself, as if one had *deceived* oneself all too long." One had hoped to *achieve* something through one's actions, "and now one realizes that becoming aims at *nothing* and achieves *nothing.*"

Nihilism "as a psychological state is reached, *secondly,*" he writes, "when one has posited a totality," an organization, a unity "in all events, and underneath all events," so that a man will have "a deep feeling of standing in the context of, and being dependent on, some whole that is infinitely superior to him." This whole need not be God, but it is, at least, some scheme like that of progress, or the advance of science, or the fate of civilization, all of which function as some form of deity.[14] "But, behold, there is no such universal! At bottom, man has lost the faith in his own value when no infinitely valuable whole works through him; i.e., he conceived such a whole *in order to be able to believe in his own value.*"

The experience of nothingness has yet a third and last form:

The Experience of Nothingness

Given these two insights, that becoming has no goal and that underneath all becoming there is no grand unity in which the individual could immerse himself completely as in an element of supreme value, an escape remains: to pass sentence on this whole world of becoming as a deception and to invent a world beyond it, a *true* world. Having reached this standpoint, one grants the reality of becoming as the *only* reality, forbids oneself every kind of clandestine access to afterworlds and false divinities—*but cannot endure this world though one does not want to deny it.*

What has happened, at bottom? The feeling of valuelessness was reached with the realization that the overall character of existence may not be interpreted by means of the concept of an "aim," the concept of "unity," or the concept of "truth." Existence has no goal or end; any comprehensive unity in the plurality of events is lacking: the character of existence is not "true," is *false.* One simply lacks any reason for convincing oneself that there is a *true* world. Briefly: the categories "aim," "unity," "being," which we used to project some values into the world—we *pull out* again; so the world looks valueless.

I recognize that I put structure into my own world. Such recognition is a necessary condition of the experience of nothingness. There is no "real" world out there, given, intact, full of significance. Consciousness is constituted by random, virtually infinite barrages of experience; these experiences are indistinguishably "inner" and "outer." The mad are aware of that buzzing confusion. The sane have put structure into it.[15] Structure *is put into experience by culture and the self,* and may also be pulled out again. Sociological consciousness recognizes such an insight under the rubric of "relativism." But the experience of nothingness casts doubt, also, on the reasons and methods of sociology (and every other science or philosophy). In its light they, too, seem like useless passions. The experience of nothingness is an experience beyond the limits of reason. It arises near the borderline of insanity. It is terrifying. It makes all attempts at speaking of purpose, goals, aims, meaning, importance, conformity, harmony, unity—it makes all such attempts seem doubtful and spurious. The person gripped by the experience of nothingness sees nearly everything *in reverse image.* What other persons call certain, he sees as pretend; what other persons call pragmatic or effective, he sees as a most ironical delusion. There is no real world out there, he says. Within human beings and outside them, there is only a great darkness, in which momentary beams of attention flash like fireflies. The experience of nothingness is an awareness of the multiplicity and polymorphousness of experience, and of the tide urging the conscious self to shape its own confusion by projecting myths.

Most people, of course, are instructed by their parents, schools, churches, economic and social roles, and other instruments of culture to shape their inner and outer confusion in clear, direct ways. A person who is "well brought up" is balanced, well adjusted, well rounded, purposive, dutiful, clear in his aims, views, and values. The well-brought-up person has been sheltered from the experience of nothingness. His feet are planted on solid ground. His perceptions of himself, others, and the world have been duly arranged.[16] For him the question of reality has been settled. That is real which his culture says is real; that is of value which his culture values. His convictions about the aim of life have been formed in him by his culture. What he is to perceive and experience in life is determined in advance, and he *will* not allow himself to perceive or to experience otherwise.

To choose against the culture is not merely to disobey; it is to "die." Against what the culture knows is real, true, and good, one has chosen the evil, the false, and the unreal. To be or not to be, that is the question. To choose against the culture is to experience nothingness.

Nihilism is an ideological interpretation imposed on the experience of nothingness. Most writers on nihilism have placed the experience of nothingness in opposition to the values of the culture, as though that experience were a threat to it.[17] I want to argue that the power of the experience of nothingness has been misperceived. Its root and source have not been detected, or else have been wrongly identified. The experience of nothingness was so new, so powerful, and so unexpected that it arrived *inconnu.* All who have since reflected upon it stand in the debt of Nietzsche and Heidegger, Freud and Sartre, but in probing for its source and power no one has yet driven an arrow into the center of the circle. The unassimilable horror of the regime of Adolf Hitler showed that the experience of nothingness may be put to the most horrible uses; the experience of nothingness may be murderous.[18] Nevertheless, the experience of nothingness is now the point from which nearly every reflective man begins his adult life. We have seen too much blood to be astonished that Hitlers are possible. History, Hegel said, is a butcher's bench.

Still, the sorrows of this century have distorted our reflections on the experience of nothingness. That experience leads not only to murder; it is also the source of creativity and plenitude. We need not avert our eyes from the nihilism of the Fascists, or evade the ambiguities of nothingness. We can also reflect upon the preconditions and fertile possibilities of that experience, which in any case already occupies our hearts.

The source of the experience of nothingness lies in the deepest recesses of human consciousness, in its irrepressible tendency to ask questions. The necessary condition for the experience of nothingness is that everything can be questioned. Whatever the presuppositions of a culture or a way of life, questions can be addressed against them and other alternatives can be imagined. Whatever the massive solidity of institutions, cultural forms, or basic symbols, accurately placed questions can shatter their claims upon us. The drive to ask questions is the most persistent and basic drive of human consciousness. It is the principle of the experience of nothingness. By exercising that drive, we come to doubt the definitions of the real, the true, and the good that our culture presents to us. Without this drive, cultural change would not be possible. What was sacred once would for all time be locked in unchanging sacredness.

Because it is the principle of cultural change, the experience of nothingness is ambiguous, for cultural change is in itself of dubious value. Because it lies so near to madness, the experience of nothingness is a dangerous, possibly destructive experience. But when it leads to changes in cultural or personal consciousness that are liberating and joyful, it is called, deservedly, a "divine madness." Those whom the city must put to death for corrupting its youth sometimes fire the consciousness of many others with a madness that comes to define a new sanity, a corruption that becomes a new morality, a nothingness that yields a new being. And then the process may begin again.

When, meanwhile, the drive to raise questions makes us aware of its total range and depth, a feeling of formlessness, or nausea, or lassitude arises. When I perceive the drive to question in its purity, apart from the products to which it leads me, I perceive the ambiguity of my own conscious life. I recognize the formlessness, the aimlessness, and the disunity implicit in my own insignificance, my mortality, my ultimate dissolution. I peer into madness, chaos, and death. These insights are true insights. Not to experience them is to evade the character of one's own consciousness. It is to live a lie. The experience of nothingness bears the taste of honesty.

The truth of the human situation, however, remains to be decided. Is the character of human consciousness so inherently chaotic that the only genuine way to mirror our situation is insanity? Quite possibly. I wish to argue tentatively that the character of human consciousness is merely tragic; that is, that the experience of nothingness may be absorbed in full sanity; that a clear and troubling recognition of our fragility, our mortality, and our ignorance need not subvert our relation to the world in which we find ourselves. The experience of nothingness may lead either to madness or to wisdom. The man who shares it, however wise, appears to those who do not share it (and sometimes to himself) as mad. Wisdom lies on the edge of insanity, just as those who wish to see themselves as sane and well adjusted in this bloody and absurd world may be foolish and insane. Our lives seem to be tragic rather

15

than absurd, but I am far from certain on that point. The issue falls one way rather than the other only by a hair.

4. The Four Myths of the University

"Even within nihilism," Albert Camus wrote in 1940, "it is possible to find the means to proceed beyond nihilism."[19] Today in Rio de Janeiro children are starving. While in San Francisco children lie on laundered sheets, in Vietnam others lie in pools of blood. The earth is rich enough so that no one has to starve, and men are not obliged to murder one another. Exactly in proportion as we are free men, we are responsible for the social, economic, and political practices of our nation that terminate in uncounted deaths.[20] Occasionally we lift our eyes from our daily routine and glimpse briefly the worldwide consequences of the American way of life. The structure of rationalization collapses.[21] We went to bed imagining ourselves decent and good; we awake to find blood on our hands. Camus wrote: "Every action today leads to murder, direct or indirect."[22]

The experience of nothingness always arises in contrast to the values of a culture. To understand the character of the experience of nothingness in America, therefore, we must penetrate the foundations of the American way of life. One culture differs from another according to the constellation of myths that shapes its attention, its attitudes, and its practices. No culture perceives human experience in a universal, direct way; each culture selects from the overwhelming experience of being human certain salient particulars. One culture differs from another in the meaning it attaches to various kinds of experience, in its image of the accomplished man, in the stories by which it structures its perceptions.[23]

Of course, men are not fully aware that their own values are shaped by myths. Myths are what men in other cultures believe in; in our own culture we deal with reality. In brief, the word "myth" has a different meaning depending upon whether one speaks of other cultures or of one's own. When we speak of others, a myth is the set of stories, images, and symbols by which human perceptions, attitudes, values, and actions are given shape and significance. When we speak of our own culture, the ordinary sense of reality performs the same function. In order to identify the myths of one's own culture, therefore, it suffices to ask: "What constitutes my culture's sense of reality?"

In the United States, as elsewhere, the issue is complicated because several versions of reality are in competition. Academic persons and artists criticize the myths of the ordinary people of America: their religiousness, their chauvinism in foreign policy, their prejudices in domestic affairs, their commercialism, their need to be boosters, and the like. Moreover, ordinary people are quick to discern that intellectuals do not share the assumptions, viewpoints, and values of the people. The intellectuals do not believe that the people see things as they are; the people do not believe that the intellectuals have their feet on the ground. What one group calls moral, the other believes the depth of immorality; what one calls patriotic, the other calls treasonous. Social, political, religious, and educational differences intensify the gap between the intellectuals and the people.[24] Instead of entering the dispute between these two shifting senses of reality, however, I would like to construct a third. It will be more helpful in defining this third myth to contrast it to the myths that dominate the American university rather than to the myths of the people. Criticism of the people is too easy; criticism of the university, until recently, has been seldom attempted.

Four basic stories shape the sense of reality in leading American universities. The first is the story of enlightenment through hardheaded, empirical intelligence (and in psychology through behavioral methods). The second is the story of the solitary, autonomous individual. The third is the story of achievement through arduous competitive work. And the fourth is the story of working within the system and concentrating upon one's own functional tasks until recognition comes. The most realistic man, in the eyes of the university circles I am describing, would be a hardnosed scholar, whose "lonely and heretical toil" (warmly supported by his colleagues) challenged the values of the community, but who persevered until the system itself turned and rewarded him with a Nobel Prize. Let us take up each strand of the myth separately.

The first means of giving structure to life is to place one's trust in empirical reason and behavioral methods. The decision to attempt to speak "objectively" and in "value-free discourse" is a decision to abstract from the thick, complex stream of life. So is the decision to study behavior rather than experience; that is, to observe actions from "outside," and to distrust the introspective view of the one who experiences the actions from "within." So is the decision to treat all issues, even human issues, analytically and quantitatively.[25] Moreover, the stream of life does not come to us ready-made for such abstraction.

It takes a great many years of rigorous socialization to make a scientist out of a young man or woman, and neophytes must be initiated into the difficult language, procedures, and viewpoints required for successful performance. Most laymen cannot understand the speech or the disciplined, technical behavior of experts. But the employment of the techniques of objective reason for the last several generations has generated power: napalm, atomic bombs, gases and chemicals that can incapacitate or destroy the human nervous system, personality, or body, and genetic mutants and machines that may develop into creatures more able and more flexible than human beings. The speech and actions of the astronauts under pressure have given us a televised demonstration of the "new type of man"; it is not a type that is wholly admirable.

The decision to choose scientific methods and, in particular, behavioral methods as a way of life is first of all *to select* certain features of human life (clarity, quantifiability, function, instrumentality) from among others. It is, secondly, *to evade* other sorts of questions and values, and thus to rig the meaning of "fact." And it is, thirdly, *to make a political choice.* Behavioral science is far from value-free; it is certainly not power-free, and someone somewhere will use the power it generates to secure his own interests. In the United States, the federal government willingly pays the incomes of sixty-five per cent of all scientists and engineers by direct or indirect subsidy. The uses to which scientific and technological work are put, and the direction of inquiry and research, are governed by political considerations.[26]

The second myth is that of the solitary autonomous individual. One of the most effective ways to manipulate men is to isolate them: "Divide and conquer." More effective still is to isolate them, while convincing them that their isolation is really their strength, and that rugged individualism is their chief protection against tyranny. In this respect, the Anglo-American tradition has perpetrated one of the coolest frauds in political history. Millions of Englishmen and Americans, divided against their fellows, believe themselves to be autonomous and free, while all the while giving evidence in their schools, their dress, their economic practices, and their habits of life of the most striking forms of docility, social conformity, and amenability to political control.[27] As the decline of English and American society continues, our former notions of superiority in these respects over Latin, French, Germanic, African, and Asian cultures are suitably humbled. Young people who serve in the Peace Corps or elsewhere experience "culture shock" on discovering that "underdeveloped" people are in many ways more fully developed than any Americans they know: in the subtlety and range of their emotions, in their sensitivities in human interaction, in their capacity to endure pain, in their skepticism regarding authority, and so on.

The myth of empirical reason has alienated many Americans from their own experience, leading them to think of themselves as objective minds. The myth of the autonomous individual has alienated many from their fellows and led them to think of themselves as atomic bits of private consciousness, turreted and protected against the encroachments of others. Thus unnaturally isolated, many experience as a leading characteristic of American life a poignant loneliness. Many imagine that their most urgent personal need is for security and status. In England and America we boast of democracy and free enterprise. But we are neither as free nor as united as we imagine ourselves; on the contrary, we are isolated, conformist, and manipulated.

The third major myth in leading universities is the need for hard, competitive work. Perhaps no other myth in our society is so painstakingly reinforced from birth—by story and example, exhortation and practice, the contriving of roles and direct schooling—as the value of hard, competitive work.[28] Without that myth, our society is inconceivable; its contradiction threatens society's very foundations. So powerful is that myth in shaping American experience and perception, that it is virtually impossible for Americans to understand how achievement is possible under any other system. Jules Henry gives the following example of how the myth is taught:

Boris had trouble reducing 12/16 to the lowest terms, and could only get as far as 6/8. The teacher asked him quietly if that was as far as he could reduce it. She suggested he "think." Much heaving up and down and waving of hands by the other children, all frantic to correct him. Boris pretty unhappy, probably mentally paralyzed. The teacher quiet, patient, ignores the others and concentrates with look and voice on Boris. After a minute or two she turns to the class and says, "Well, who can tell Boris what the number is?" A forest of hands appears, and the teacher calls Peggy. Peggy says that four may be divided into the numerator and the denominator.

Henry remarks:

Boris's failure made it possible for Peggy to succeed; his misery is the occasion for her rejoicing. This is a standard condition of the contemporary American elementary school. To a Zuni, Hopi or Dakota Indian, Peggy's performance would seem cruel beyond belief, for competition, the wringing of success from somebody's failure, is a form of torture foreign to those noncompetitive cultures. Looked at from Boris's point of view, the nightmare at the blackboard was, perhaps, a lesson in controlling himself so that he would not fly shrieking from the room under enormous public pressure. Such experiences force every man reared in our culture, over and over again, night in, night out, even at the pinnacle of success, to dream not of success, but of failure. In school the external nightmare is internalized for life. Boris was not learning arithmetic only; he was learning the *essential nightmare also. To be successful in our culture one must learn to dream of failure.*[29]

Apart from motives of competition, there are many motives for action, for self-realization, for supreme achievement, and for overcoming scarcity. And even competition may be conceived in two ways. A friend of mine witnessed a brilliant soccer match in southern France. Afterward, he congratulated the captain of the winning team for having won. The French peasant was embarrassed. One does not congratulate a man for "winning"; the point of the competition was not to vanquish the other side but, by facing worthy opponents, to force oneself to new levels of exertion.

In America, the emphasis on "success" dramatized by Miss America contests, bowl games, television quizzes, and spelling bees dehumanizes human performance; atomic individual is set over against atomic individual, and it is not the worth of their performance that is honored but the mere, almost independent fact of the success of one of them. Success is perceived as luck, a grace, a gift; failure as the lot of the damned. The myth of success renders useless the concept of internal worth, and countless Americans seem to feel insecure, helpless, and worthless when the lottery of success has not selected them. Even the notion that one must work hard in order to be worthy of success is commonly absorbed into the syntax of success: one works hard, not with the sense of dignity that comes from inner growth, risk and expansion, but with the hope of a vindication from beyond. The myth of competitive work is seldom oriented toward an internal sense of dignity; it is other-regarding, outwardly expectant, full of foreboding. An astonishing number of intelligent students, who should know better, want to satisfy two myths at once: *both* to study what is of in-

21

trinsic value to themselves *and* to get an "A."

The fourth way of life in the university emphasizes working within the system. The trap that a pragmatic, empirical way of life sets for itself grows from its refusal to question its own presuppositions, goals, values, or methods. The empiricist or pragmatist deals with answerable questions and measurable results. He defines "reality" according to what is "realizable" by his methods and in terms of the given situation; he concentrates upon clear next steps.[30] He cannot be bothered with "theological" or "metaphysical" speculation about experience, values, or long-range goals. In an important paper on the quest for peace in Vietnam, for example, Henry A. Kissinger describes in detail how realistic American bureaucrats fail to comprehend, and dislike dealing with, fundamental realities, basic issues, and long-range goals. They prefer dealing with daily, pragmatic, functional issues.[31] (Kissinger does not, himself, escape the limitations of realism.[32])

Realism effectively makes one a participant in the ongoing system. It stifles the revolutionary, utopian, visionary impulse. It teaches one compromise, patience, and acquiescence. It rewards dissent that strengthens the system, not dissent directed at the heart of the system or insisting on the construction of a significantly new system. There is compelling evidence that realistic social and political reforms do not, in fact, alter power arrangements or weaken key interest groups in our society; political symbols change, but the same elites remain in unchallenged power.[33]

A precise analysis of American society shows that the analysis of myths, rituals, and symbols touches the heart of American reality much more accurately than the analysis of the pragmatist.[34] The pragmatist likes to believe that hardheaded, factual, toughminded analysis, in quantifiable terms, will change American society (and the world?) more effectively than any alternative. But the more the pragmatist has his way, the more hardened and obtuse the American system becomes. (Some Americans would call it progress to turn the whole world into an extended New Jersey.) The choice of the pragmatist myth of "working within the system" is not value-free; to assure oneself of this, it suffices to call that choice the radical disease from which we suffer. Many will leap to its defense as normal, ordinary, and inevitable. They will do so with passion.

Perhaps I have said enough about the central stories that shape American life. Americans, like all other peoples in history, live by myths because human beings have no other choice. Experience rushes in upon us in such floods that we must break it down, select from it, abstract, shape, and relate. A culture is constituted by the meaning it imposes on human experience.[35] It imposes that meaning by every means at its disposal, and by so doing it shapes human life into a manageable sequence. A culture comes into being and endures through its ability to create a myth. The experience of nothingness is the origin of all mythmaking. Is it any wonder that every myth leads back to that primal experience? Culture begins and ends in the void. An honest culture does not evade its origin or its end.

5. Story, Myth, and Horizon

Contemporary studies in ethics, in Anglo-American philosophical circles, concentrate upon logic and language; I wish, instead, to concentrate upon the drive to understand and upon myths and symbols. My reason for doing so is that men seldom, if ever, act according to principles and rules stated in words and logically arranged. They act, rather, according to models, metaphors, stories, and myths. Their action is imitative rather than rule-abiding. Prior to their intention to obey sets of rules, they are trying to become a certain type of person.

Rules are to myths what single words are to sentences. The same word may have different meanings in different sentences; the same rule may be obeyed differently by men living out different myths. A man whose myth construes human life in functional, utilitarian terms may obey the rule "Keep promises" in one way; a man whose myth construes human life in terms of fidelity between human persons may obey the same rule in a quite different spirit and to a quite different effect. *The story a man is acting out determines his actions more than the verbally stated rule he is following.* To adequately analyze ethical behavior, one must pay attention to a logical category prior to the category of rules, principles, propositions, and codes of behavior—specifically, to the category of myth, story, symbol, and ritual. The latter dimension of ethical behavior is commonly overlooked in our intellectual culture because of a systematic bias that might be termed the rationalistic bias.

According to the rationalistic bias, men are primarily reasonable creatures whose behavior may be analyzed into segments that manifest a logical structure. That structure may be imagined as either cognitive or emotive. The cognitivists argue that the premises of ethical argument are derived from statements of fact and predictable consequences, while the emotivists argue that such premises are derived from emotional states like approval and disapproval.[36] In both cases, the logic of verbal argument is employed as the model for understanding ethical action. But action is fundamentally unlike argument. Effective and telling argument depends upon precise abstraction, but effective and telling action depends upon full concretion. In argument, one need only be an observer; in action, one must commit oneself to the skein of events.

A pragmatic theory of argument, to be sure, tries to lessen the distance between knowing and doing in such a way that knowing, too, is conceived as a species of action. The knower is also a doer, implicated in the tangled texture of the world he is trying to understand.[37] But insofar as the knower depends upon criteria of relevance and evidence, canons of inquiry, a model of justification, and a "quasi-conscience" by which to satisfy himself that his inquiry is valid, justified, acceptable, or the like,[38] it becomes apparent that the knower is, himself, dependent upon a basic myth. For the knower is acting out a quest. Knowing is a heuristic activity: it is goal-centered, and the achievement of the goal brings about a specific satisfaction. A man reveals himself in the things that please and displease him. If you know what sorts of achievements satisfy a knower, you can discern the story he is acting out, trace his odyssey, and gauge the temper of his spirit.

The pragmatic theory of knowing, in brief, has the structure and function of a myth. To study what a given pragmatist takes to be effective, real, and relevant is to discern the story he is acting out, the identity he imagines himself to possess, the contours of the world as he pictures it. The fact that a man abjures the word "myth" and thinks of himself as hardheaded and exclusively realistic does not count as evidence that he is not acting out a myth; on the contrary, it furnishes an index to the power of his myth over his mind.

One man's sense of reality is another man's myth. The American professor or bureaucrat who estimates the "reality" of foreign affairs according to quantitative, statistical, and other hardnosed methods may or may not be in touch with all the significant factors involved. The record of our recent past—whether we think of foreign affairs or of our own cities—is not comforting in this respect. It is entirely possible that the view of the world dominant among American professional people—in the academy, in industry, in the military, and in the government—is badly out of touch with crucial considerations, even though that view is thought to be the paradigm of nonmythical, nonideological, realistic thinking. A clue to this possibility is given by Daniel Bell, the author of *The End of Ideology* and one of the major spokesmen of academic realism. Bell writes:

The university, which is the place where theoretical knowledge is sought, tested and codified in a disinterested way, becomes the primary institution of the new society. Perhaps it is not too much to say that if the business firm was the key institution of the past one hundred years because of its role in organizing production for the mass creation of products, the university will become the central institution of the next hundred years because of its role as the new source of innovation and knowledge.[39]

If Bell is correct, then the university is becoming the chief institution in determining the American sense of reality. He suggests that the university will present us knowledge that is "sought, tested and codified *in a disinterested way.* " The university will fill in American society the place filled by the church in medieval society. It will become the chief guardian of the cultural myths. But who will guard the guardian?

In the analysis of ethical questions, it is indispensable, then, to detect and to criticize the contours of one's own realism, indispensable to become aware of the myths that shape human actions. These myths, unfortunately, operate both in intentional human acts and in unattentive, unguarded acts. If it makes sense for someone to ask: "What are you trying to do?" your action qualifies as a "human act";[40] if not, then it is the mere "act of a man."[41] For example, if during your stay on the beach someone asks you what you are trying to do, and then for the first time you notice that, absently, your toe has been pushing up a wall of sand, you may answer: "Nothing." But you may, in fact, have been trying to build a small sea wall, and in that case the question brings to light a genuine human act. Human acts, it may safely be asserted, have a base in myth; there is no human act that is not an acting out of a story. What the story is, and how dominant that story is among others in your life, may be difficult to determine. The difficulty is commensurate with the complexity of the human comedy.

Freud discovered that not only human acts, but also the "acts of men"—the routine, seemingly random, and unintended acts of our lives—also carry mythical content, and in their own way tell the story of our lives.[42] (What we are "trying to do" and what we do without trying, moreover, may belong to different and opposed myths.) Not to recognize that our own sense of reality is different from that of others, and that that sense of reality is given shape by a constellation of fundamental stories, both conscious and unconscious, is to overlook sources of illumination without which our understanding of ethics is severely impoverished.

In order to approach ethical questions without excluding in advance the dimension of myth, I would like to invoke the technical concept of "horizon" or "standpoint."[43] A horizon has two poles: the subject and the range of his activities. The point of the horizon metaphor is to link the subject and his world in a mutually defining relationship. It is to refuse to think dualistically of an isolated self over against an external world, a conscious ego trapped inside a bag of skin in a world of colliding objects. What we know of the world is known only through consciousness, and we are conscious only through being in a world. Self and world interpenetrate; neither exists in regard to the other until they are mutually united in act. One pole of my horizon is the range of all I can experience, understand, evaluate, and do. The other pole is the subject of those activities of experiencing, understanding, evaluating, doing. Neither pole can be attended to without reference to the other.

Secondly, as the subjective pole is specified by the four activities of experiencing, understanding, evaluating, and doing, so the objective pole is specified by the symbols through which those activities are given shape and effect. Institutions of culture—family, school, church, state, economic and social order—ordinarily provide us with the symbols by which we shape our activities. To ask "Who am I?" is to ask "Under what institutions am I being formed?"

Thirdly, men are both question-asking and symbol-making animals. To become certain that men ask questions, it suffices to doubt it; for to doubt is to question. And to become certain that men are symbol-makers, it suffices to notice how the clothes you wear signal to others your sex, your national and class identity, your relationship to prevailing conventions, your taste, and your self-image.

Because men are question-making animals, their horizon is dynamic. To shatter any given set of symbols and to clamor for others they may raise doubts, shift presuppositions, or redirect their attention and interest. The question-asking drive establishes the possibility of development.

Because men are symbol-making animals, they can structure their superabundant, polymorphous experiences and assimilate them in perceptual forms. They can gain insight into the unities, identities, and wholes among the data of experience. They can articulate criteria and procedures of evaluation. And they can devise strategies and tactics to direct the effects of their actions. The symbol-making drive establishes the possibility of orderly and intellectually manageable development.

The value of the concept of horizon is twofold. If each man has his own unique horizon, then the self-awareness of each must include a pervasive sense of the relativity of views of reality. To work with the concept of horizon as a fundamental tool is to be constantly reminded of the central role of myth-making in all acting and knowing. Secondly, the concept of horizon is sweeping and all-inclusive; elements in the subject or in the range of his activities presently undifferentiated may at a later time be more carefully articulated.

In particular, the concept of horizon is intended to pierce the rationalistic bias by calling attention to the fundamental role of undifferentiated, inexhaustible experience. Thus, dreams and fantasies and zany impressions and impulses of all sorts, which quite clearly play a role in ethical action, cannot a priori be excluded from consideration. Secondly, the notion of horizon emphasizes that social and institutional forces structure the perceptions, feelings and intentions of the would-be rationalistic agent.

In a certain sense, the concept of horizon is antihumanistic, for it does not suppose that ethical action is wholly conscious or wholly self-originated. On the contrary, the concept of horizon emphasizes that the self and its world interpenetrate at every point. There is no part that is purely self or purely world. It may well be the case that both reality and the self are social constructs; that is, that who I am and what I imagine the world to be like are constantly being shaped for me by the society of which I am a part. My world is not wholly distinguishable from the twentieth-century educated American world; my self is not wholly distinguishable from the social groups in which I live and move and gain my being. It is truer to say, not

most people, what their culture accepts as reality *is* reality; their culture's sudden loss of confidence, credibility, and unity disorients them. The aim, structure, and value that the culture had put into existence for them have, in Nietzsche's metaphor, been pulled out. Many persons in the culture, of course, including many of high intelligence, continue to support the prevailing but already collapsing myths.[2] Leaders make urgent appeals for a renewed sense of purpose, a return to sources, a rededication to original values. Yet in the United States, for example, an articulate fraction of the population no longer believes in the American way of life: not in competitiveness, not in America's moral goodness, not in the automatic blessings of progress, not in the veracity of even the highest public officials, not in the people's basic decency or commitment to democracy.

Widely established myths do not commonly come crashing down all at once. Basic myths so comprehensively shape one's view of reality that one can hardly get outside them. Thus, in the United States, many who have been disillusioned about the meaning of American life continue to try to reform the network of its institutions; many others, who have despaired entirely of "the system," continue to judge it by peculiarly American presuppositions. The latter demand an innocence and justice of American institutions that few other nationals would dream of demanding of any institution. They lack a sense for the tangled, evil, ambiguous past (their personal history included). They expect a utopian future, made by their own hands. They are scarcely aware of their own moral ambivalence and corruption. Many of the practitioners of "radical" politics recapitulate the basic myths—often the most blind and destructive ones—traditional to Americans.

Widely established myths shape not only the direction, depth, and the expectations of an outlook, but also its perception of threats and contradictions. A pragmatist understands very well why existentialists think ill of certain pragmatic doctrines and practices; it is due to flaws in the existentialists, to *their* lack of clear thinking and solidity. A Russian Communist is not disturbed when Americans picture Russians as imperialists plotting successive takeovers; he knows that Americans have to use propaganda to mask the expansion of the American empire around the world since 1941. The loyal Russian defends the Russian invasion of Czechoslovakia just as the patriotic American defends the American invasion of the Dominican Republic. Even when he reconsiders, each man usually finds his own sense of reality, not surprisingly, reconfirmed. When challenged, each man elaborates his own view in order to absorb its contradictions, and each opposes his own firm sense of reality to the other person's mere myths.[3]

In the United States there is widespread resistance to the experience of nothingness; it comes from many sources. To those Americans who have a naive belief in God, His providence, His special blessings upon America, and His support of men of progress, brotherhood, and free will, the experience of nothingness manifests a loss of faith. To the confidence man, cynical and quick, glib and always inventing new outlets for his ambition, the experience of nothingness is too serious; he runs. To those Americans who believe in the advance of science, research, and civilization—who believe, as Freud put it, in the *Logos* progressively discovered by scientists[4] —the experience of nothingness is a childish indulgence.[5] To them, men who let themselves be wounded by the experience of nothingness lack the toughness to put their shoulders to the wheel of progress. And to many committed religious and liberal persons, the experience of nothingness is symptomatic of a sick, perverse loss of nerve.

In America two great cultural myths have slowly been losing their power. How accurately do we describe ourselves by telling each other the stories of Christianity or the stories of scientific, technological progress? Can we really believe that man and the world are commensurate, in the sense that human intelligence anticipates, and explores an intelligible world?[6] Does sanity consist in becoming "realistic," well adjusted to the cosmos or at least to circumstance? Possibly it is more true that the world is so absurd that only the insane are in tune with it, and that the sane, who try to be realistic, are living a life of make-believe.

Both the Christian and the scientific stories lead us into self-images that conflict with one another and with our own actions. These stories usually lead us to imagine that we have an identifiable self, autonomous and unique, of inestimable value and dignity, and an end in itself (Kant). On the other hand, the scientific stories sometimes suggest the reverse: the self is a social construct, rarely unique, and never fully autonomous, of no special value or dignity.[7] Often I "feel" that I am of inestimable value because I am a man; at other times I feel useless and instantly expendable. Again, my "self" seems to shift, change, be converted, and assume so many shapes that I cannot be sure I have a self, or what the balance of power is between my own autonomy and the subtle influences of social setting. I can read papers on free will and be convinced by them, and papers on the social construction of the self and be similarly convinced. But when I try to become aware of my own actual experience, and try to decide who or what I am, I find none of the stories available in our culture adequate.

There are two stages in my disillusionment. The stories of Christianity about creation and man's role in nature are thrown into confusion by the stories of world process as imagined by science. The ethical problems raised by man's control over his environment, the processes of life, and the processes of consciousness are not even foreshadowed, let alone solved, by a simple appeal to the Christian stories. The metaphor "Enlightenment," favored by university people, suggests passage from a dark, mythological age into one where reality is more accurately illuminated. That passage, however, has been from one myth to another, and the second myth, like the first, has also proved to be inadequate. The university is now what the church once was, the guardian of conservative myth and the indispensable supporter of political and economic power.

The objective methods favored by scholars determine for "the enlightened" the limits of the real: what we may count as hard and secure and what we ought to distrust as soft and subjective. But an academic revolution challenges the pretensions to objectivity of liberal scholarship.[8] The academic revolution is not a matter of administrative reform or functional readjustment; it is an intellectual struggle concerned with what counts as adequate theory. It is a struggle over competing interpretations of reality.

The American character has always favored optimism, action, concrete effectiveness. At the turn of the century, Charles Sanders Peirce, William James, and John Dewey succeeded in a remarkably short time in formulating the American's instinctive sense of reality in a rather powerful philosophy called "pragmatism."[9] That philosophy became the directing spirit of American academic inquiry and instruction. Unless I am mistaken, America's encounters with other world cultures since 1940, and especially since 1960, have placed the severe limitations of our national philosophy in a scouring light. We have been obliged to face the concrete effects of courses of action undertaken in unflagging optimism: unplanned technological progress, the repression of spontaneity, the exploitation of the natural environment, imperial misadventures, the dominance over American life of the Department of Defense. The revulsion is profound. Nothing less than the orientation of the American character, the American sense of reality, the national philosophy is in question.

The American way of life has brought to the surface of daily life a basic contradiction between science and humanism. The more science and technology advance, the clearer their inner dynamic becomes. They are not directed toward the good of concrete, individual human beings but toward efficiency. The primary goal of scientific knowledge is power; the primary goal of technology is efficiency.[10] Neither power nor efficiency has a necessary relation to the integrity of persons. A modern, technological, urban environment is supposed to exemplify progress, but we lack the means to measure the physical and psychical discomfort, the uprootedness, the repression, and the ascetical routines imposed upon us by technical progress. Our educational system favors pragmatic, conventional, cognitive intelligence rather than creative, imaginative, and affective intelligence.[11] The costs in alienation are hardly measurable.

An American's sense of reality is gratified when he is being "objective," when he has the "hard facts," when "the figures" are all there in front of him. American scholars have produced thousands of mimeographed and printed monographs on Vietnam; they have counted buildings, trees, miles of road, telephones, doctors, bodies—everything that can plausibly be counted. But all that arduous counting does not guarantee that American scholars have a good grasp of Vietnamese reality. "A man of courage and determination is incommensurable," a Vietnamese officer will say, contempt for Americans in his voice, "with cowards. How can you understand by counting?" Americans think that the Vietnamese are unrealistic and mystical; Vietnamese think that the American belief in the intimate connection between the really real and the quantifiable is a very violent mysticism.

Vietnam has been an ineradicable shock to the American sense of reality. It has thrown into doubt the sense of reality that is shaped by empirical methods, statistics, and objectivity. The ideology built into "value neutrality" has been exposed. Social convulsions within the United States have further exposed the insensitivies of the American sense of reality. What is at stake is not precisely America's image of herself but rather the methods of perceiving, imagining, sensing, and understanding by which such images are reached. American realism, American pragmatism, American empiricism are suspect. They do not yield a satisfactory sense of reality, but a myth of far too narrow a range.

To be sure, the point of view of American philosophy has been under attack for some years by writers and thinkers influenced by European philosophers or by the necessities and methods of creative art. Charles Frankel, for example, felt obliged to answer such accusations in *The Case For Modern Man* and in such essays as "Existentialism, or Cosmic Hypochondria," "The Anti-intellectualism of the Intellectuals," and "The Love of Anxiety."[12] But since the racial struggle and the Vietnam war, fresh accusations have been laid against pragmatic, objective scholarship.[13]

2. Three Doubts About Objectivity

In general, earlier critics like Buber, Weber, Tillich, Sartre, Heidegger, and others attacked the lack of reverence, metaphysical wonder, and sense of mystery in empirical, pragmatic objectivity. They asserted that the American sense of reality was too matter-of-fact, automatic, and functional; that American scientists and intellectuals accepted the limitations of human reason as they accepted the limitations of a piece of machinery; thus they had lost an appropriate admiration for the human person.[14] The new accusations are usually based on the political and social implications of scholarly objectivity. The chief point of these accusations is that there is no political or social vacuum within which objectivity is possible.

The new accusations against the theory and practice of objectivity fall into three categories: objectivity as a psychological state of mind, objectivity as a scholarly project, and objectivity as the form of a sociopolitical system. These accusations are not attacks upon intelligence, accurate understanding, or good judgment but upon the myth of objectivity as a too-narrow expression of reason, which leaves out of consideration too many delicate but crucial operations of human intelligence. Widely accepted accounts of scientific method, the argument runs, accounts that emphasize the impersonal, mechanical procedures of inquiry, and that as much as possible rule out the human subject, as a source of error, are mistaken accounts of what happens in the employment of scientific method.[15] A more adequate sense of reality, a new intellectual method, must be established.

The first step toward that goal is to recognize that objectivity is a psychological state. It is difficult to acquire and difficult to maintain, and it depends upon the support of a social environment. It is incontestable, Frankel writes "that objectivity is a rare individual trait, and that even those who do achieve objectivity do so with great difficulty and maintain it usually only for brief periods of time. . . . Objectivity in thought and judgment, generally speaking, is a social achievement, the product of long cooperative processes of controlled questioning, communication, and mutual criticism."[16] In a paradoxical way, then, objectivity requires the cultivation of specific subjective states, the disciplining of attention and selected habits of thought, the screening out of other sources of consciousness, control over emotions, and a commitment to private and public honesty, to care and precision, to technical statement and social cooperation. Objectivity is a highly selective, highly developed, subjective state. It is the selection of one set of values in preference to others, the shaping of perception and other mental operations along specified lines, and the establishment of social means of verification.

Objectivity, in short, has the logical status of a myth: it builds up one sense of reality rather than others. It is a myth whose attainment and maintenance demand of its subjects a rigorous and continual asceticism; its disciplines lay great demands upon human emotions, affections, and fantasies. James Watson's *The Double Helix* gives the lie to the myth of objectivity, as does the work of other scientists like Loren Eiseley.[17] But students who wish to give their lives to this myth through careers in science or technology are often taught that they must learn to censor flights of fancy, dreams, impulses, wishes, preferences, instincts, and spontaneities of many sorts, to do so not only occasionally but habitually, and not only in their immediate professional activities but for long supporting stretches of their lives as well. Science and technology ask of their practitioners a whole way of life for which young people must be socialized by many years of schooling.

The bland psychology of astronauts is a caricature of the result-ant way of life. Watches on their wrists, precise schedules, analytic thinking, prescribed laboratory exercises, and other conditioners tie our young people into the scientific, technological culture of which they are members. The schools prearrange their experiences and perceptions, inculcating a value-free, pragmatic, one-dimen-sional frame of reference.[18] Students are taught to minimize or ignore their own experiences, perceptions, emotions, and imagina-tions. Confrontation with or development of the following are ex-cluded: spirit, soul, sexual desire, contemplation, daydreaming, bloodshed, violence, moral integrity, bodily processes, utopian schemes, myth, subjectivity, ritual, the refusal to "adjust" to scien-tific democracy, and the like.

We are not compelled to accept any one psychological state as our only access to reality. Objectivity is not the only reasonable state of mind; it is not even a good description of scientific or technical thinking. Most of what we call thinking goes on sublimi-nally; most of our understanding, our comparing, and our inventing spring from that preconscious stream in which experiences, fanta-sies, metaphors, affects, and images mix together in fertile combina-tions.[19] Insofar as the objective mind is thought to be impersonal, detached, analytic, verbal, precise, and clear, the theory of objec-tivity represents only a part of human judgment.

A more adequate theory, as many scientists are the first to em-phasize, would have to account for the importance of "the preconscious stream" to invention, discovery, and concrete comprehension; and it would have to note that objectivity is not so much impersonal as interpersonal. We escape from the limitations of our own biases and predilections not by making ourselves as machine-like as possible, but by entering as thoroughly as possible into public and social argument with our fellows. The word "objec-tive," in fact, is misleading; we do not seek to be impersonal non-subjects, but to deepen and to engage our subjectivity with that of others. When we are at our most reasonable, we not only seek to

38

fix concepts with precision, but also to raise further questions beyond the range of our present clarities. Thus it is as important to promote imaginations flexible enough to alter the presuppositions of existing analytic schemes as it is to promote analytic intelligence. Precision is often useful; ambiguity is often creative.

The myth of objectivity leads to similar misunderstandings in American journalism. Vice President Agnew and President Nixon exemplified the American myth in 1969 when they requested news commentators to separate editorial comment from the objective reporting of facts. But there are no facts "out there" apart from human observers. And human observers become not more, but less astute when they try to be neutral. It is important for reporters to understand and to sympathize with a wide range of points of view. Largeness of mind and soul (generated, perhaps, by the experience of nothingness) is the primary virtue of the newscaster. But largeness of mind and soul is quite different from a pretended objectivity. For a pretended objectivity serves the establishment, the well off, and particularly the government.[20]

A modern government has access to the news media at all hours of the day and night. In the United States, it is assumed that government officials are speaking the truth until the opposite can be proven, and they are seldom if every vigorously challenged or cross-examined in public. Merely "objective" or "neutral" reporting, therefore, immeasurably strengthens the hand of government. The public hears the government's point of view, which is treated respectfully, even with a certain awe and restraint, and then commented on as if it were an example of reasonable discourse. Yet the American people—even members of the Senate, in closed session —were lied to about the Gulf of Tonkin incident in 1964. And a flagrantly untrue account of the origins of the Vietnam war has been voiced again and again by more than one American President.

It would be much more healthy if Americans assumed, now that television has made government propaganda so powerful, that their government is always lying or, at the very least, coloring the truth.

Government officials should not be allowed to appear on television or to have their comments covered in the press without instant rebuttal by opponents with other viewpoints. To cover propaganda with the mantle of neutrality is to strengthen the powers of conformity.

Reporters and newscasters know that if they aim at objectivity, at presenting "the facts" without "editorializing," they run the risk of giving dignity to nonsense, drivel, and outright lies. What really happened in an event is not, they know, discovered by some neutral observation machine, not even by a camera. Events are not events until they are interpreted by human beings. To present events "without interpretation" or "without editorial comment" is, in fact, to interpret them according to criteria that are not likely to shed light on what the events really were. To list statistics, or outwardly observable happenings, or quotations from witnesses, is to give a very narrow view of the human world. It is to offer interpretation and editorial comment of a very misleading sort. Reality does not come divided into "facts" and "interpretation."

The model for good reporting, then, is not objectivity but largemindedness. The experience of nothingness should liberate a reporter from feeling the need to appear impersonal. He does not have to report to us merely his own feelings and prejudices. At his best, he walks around events, showing us more than one interpretation of them, using his own skills as an interpreter to portray deep and subtle nuances of various points of view. At his best, for example, a reporter does not merely repeat the shocking rhetoric of a Viet Cong or North Vietnamese spokesman; he also tries to show why the Viet Cong or North Vietnamese thinks as he does. He understands that most of the television news focuses on upper or middle class environments and on figures from elite groups; Americans are seldom shown the world from the point of view of the poor. Good reporting enters into many different viewpoints; it is pluralistically subjective. The pursuit of objectivity, by contrast, comforts and confirms the establishment in its own sense of reality. The statistics of power are, objectively, stacked on its side.

The second step in establishing a new sense of reality is to recognize that scholarly projects have social and political implications. What to study, how to study it, under whose sponsorship, and for whose benefit—each of these questions involves the scholar in value choices. Research directed to military use quite obviously involves a political commitment. But so also do anthropological studies of underground and nonelite groups, as do sociological studies designed to raise questions important to the middle class, to industrialists, to government, or to the poor. The number of inquiries that can be made is unlimited. To choose this one rather than that one as a focal point for one's energies and talents, and to accept social rewards in wages and prestige for so doing, is to make a choice of sociopolitical import. Such choices are not neutral, indifferent, or value-free.

Often the choices are complex, and the exact sociopolitical bearing of a given research project is difficult to determine. Scholarly discourse is in itself a long-term social good, even though it is limited to privileged elites; it would be a disservice to society to limit scholars to schemes of relevance currently popular in the society. The point remains that scholars stand upon the backs of the poor and the dispossessed; they are members of a privileged class among men. What they do with their liberty is of concern to all their brothers.

In proportion as the political fruits of science and technology have grown immense, so also have the moral implications of every intellectual project. A distinction between morality and technology has never been valid, but it certainly is not valid now. The crucial technological question is no longer: "Can we do x?" but "Should we do x?" Simply to do x may be to squander time and resources desperately needed elsewhere. As Werner Heisenberg notes: "For the first time in the course of history man on earth faces only himself, he finds no longer any other partner or foe. . . . In earlier epochs man saw himself opposite nature. . . . [But now] we invariably encounter structures created by man, so that in a sense we always meet only ourselves."[21] We used to think that almost any new invention or fresh discovery was automatically humanistic. We could speak of "progress" without qualification.

In earlier times man was endangered by wild animals, disease, hunger, cold, and other forces of nature, and in this strife every extension of technology represented a strengthening of his position and therefore progress. In our time, when the earth is becoming ever more densely settled, the narrowing of the possibilities of life and thus the threat to man's existence originates above all from other people, who also assert their claim to the goods of the earth. In such a confrontation, the extension of technology need no longer be an indication of progress.[22]

Objectivity is, thirdly, the informing spirit of our capitalistic, planned economy, our social order, and our political institutions. Hundreds of thousands of experts and technicians are needed to run the mass media, the universities, the government bureaus, the industries, the armies, and the farms of the nation. The university is the mainstay of the entire system, and thus has acquired immense political importance. A technological society, moreover, needs to plan, and to organize its own development so that huge expenditures for research and development today will adequately meet the needs of tomorrow.[23] A powerfully conservative, manipulative bias is thus given to the entire system. Technical novelty is celebrated, but access to basic resources and future markets must be carefully prearranged. A relatively stable world order is a prerequisite. Thus the delicate plans required by a highly developed technology shape the social and political order.

Questions that appear to be merely technical and value-free are in fact mirror images of the men who raise them. What such men see as alternatives become alternatives; questions which they ignore go unasked. Even value-free, technical game analysis is mythical and hence value-laden. For to imagine this scenario and to ignore that one, to raise this possibility and not that, is to select one's own range of possibilities: to project one's own values and image upon the future. Raising questions about the future has most serious sociopolitical consequences. Hence, the questions, "Which questions *ought* we to ask? Which alternatives *ought* we to consider?," have become, as their form suggests, profoundly ethical questions.

In these three ways, the pursuit of objectivity, value-free discourse, and pragmatic description apart from moral issues is less than convincing as a way of life. Persons who claim to speak objectively and technically in abstraction from moral and political considerations, are exemplars of bad faith. For whatever their conscious intentions, their activities involve them in moral and political commitments. Established interests could not grind on in their relentless way without them. Their claims to detachment and disinterestedness are belied by the salaries paid them and the deference shown them.

When professors, for example, claim to speak not in their own personal voice, but in the name of science or of their professional discipline, their attempt at impersonality places them in the position of mouthpieces, not of men. Professors, indeed, are often tempted to play the role, "Reasonable, Objective, Unimpassioned Man." Such a pretense often prompts many students to charge their professors with a peculiar, specific form of evasion: moral and political choice under the cover of value-free discourse. "How do you know," they say, "when you are hearing your professor's own voice as a man, and when merely the professional part of him? When are we ever exposed to hearing a man speak as a man?"

One cannot assume that objective scholarship as currently practiced in American universities assists the progress of the human race rather than parochially American (white, middle class American) purposes. Scholarship has latent as well as manifest functions. A man's life work, despite his conscious intentions, reinforces values of certain sorts and ignore others, and operates within one set of cultural myths and ignores others. It is all too easy to claim to be cosmopolitan, humanistic, and universal when one's frame of reference is in fact racially and culturally parochial.

Thus the myth of objectivity shows ragged edges today. In *Soul on Ice*, Eldridge Cleaver remarks that the year 1954 was a watershed because it launched two vast cultural movements: the Supreme Court decision ordered desegregation, with the legal result that white and black integration might proceed. And Chubby Checkers began to perform the "twist," with the social result that whites could begin to live in their bodies as blacks always have in theirs.[24] The "twist" marked the beginning of the end of the mind-body split; even "the Charleston" was, by contrast, formal and disciplined by mind. The "twist" permitted millions of young people all around the world to act out the death of cerebral objectivity and to develop a sensibility and imagination that required a more adequate theory of perception and judgment. For the ways of perception and feeling never lost by the poor and the dispossessed of the world are once again becoming accessible, through travel and intercultural penetration, to those whose minds were patterned to objectivity and analytic reason.

Technology itself calls forth a new sense of reality. The films taken by American astronauts who circled the moon showed us Earth as a small blue-brown planet in the infinitude of space. The vivid image reinforced our growing perception of human beings as a single distinct race. Races of biological mutants or thinking machines might grow more powerful than men and make us slaves.[25] Such a nightmare sharpens our identity. We need a philosophy adequate to a new sense of our own humanity and commensurate with the music that already shapes the sensibilities of virtually all the young people of the world.

3. The Drive to Raise Questions

When dominant myths are shattered by fresh experiences, whose onrush they cannot contain, countless persons who accepted those myths as reality suddenly share the experience of nothingness. The values and sense of reality proper to the receding world are not adequate to the civilization that arises all around them; hence, pervasive despair and anomie. Cultural conditions, then, make the experience of nothingness more frequent. But something within each individual man makes that experience possible. The source of the experience of nothingness lies in man's unstructured, relentless drive to ask questions. That source has too long been overlooked, possibly out of fascination with the melancholy intensity of the experience itself, possibly because that drive is so much a part of every inquiry that inquirers commonly take it for granted. Bernard Lonergan was the first philosopher to take that drive seriously and to give it primacy in his philosophical reflection.[26] What I hope to add is a stress on its nonverbal, nonintellectual character.

The drive to question manifests itself in our behavior under many guises. In its simplest form it is the tendency to attend, to notice, to differentiate. In the child, the drive to question reveals itself in the delight at being held and cuddled, in the pleasure of touching and tasting, in sensual and affective exploration. All of these are contacts beyond the organism itself, essential for the child's future boldness. Later, the drive to question is found in the child's delight with words, pictures, names, and the playful back-and-forth interchange of newly learned symbols and newly differentiated experiences.

Fundamentally, the drive to question is a sort of open-mouthed hunger of attending, noticing, doubting. It is not only a superficial curiosity; it is a hunger to become-one-with. An ancient name for it is intentionality; it is a sort of focusing of consciousness, a tending toward. But it is an infinitely resourceful sort of focusing, able to change perspective, angle, direction, depth, intensity; able, too, to double back upon its own operations and to alter its own performance. Indeed, its capacity to double back upon itself—the capacity of the drive to question to question itself—is what makes it the source of the experience of nothingness.

When persons pull back the values, structures, and aims they had put into their experience, they often perceive themselves as unstructured, formless, and free. If the theories of pragmatism, realism, and objectivity are no longer to be believed, can anything be solid? It would be more accurate to say that we are so formed that the drive to question can lead us to cast doubt upon the structures we inherit from our culture, to criticize them, to modify and rearrange and to some extent replace them.[27]

The drive to question is a peculiar kind of form. It is supple and protean and without content; it is without limits or constrictions or shapes of its own. It is free to take any shape, susceptible to the unique forming appropriate to each sort of content. It can approach various contents experimentally, from fresh angles, with fresh expectations. The accuracy of its approach can become increasingly appropriate to the content in question.

The drive to question cannot operate without assuming some concrete form (raising this question rather than that, restlessly nudging attention this way rather than that). But there is no concrete form whatever that it cannot, sooner or later, challenge, undercut, revise, replace. The drive to question operates through every stage of awareness: through dreams, images, experiences, perceptions, orientations, conceptions, theorizing, decisions, and actions. Insofar as these moments of awareness can be ordered among themselves in various ways, the drive to question may also be directed in different sequences and complex combinations.

Without experience, the images I have of love are thin and uncomplicated. When my images run in a romantic direction only, even the concept of a realistic, mature love may elude me. When my conceptions are fuzzy, my judgments can scarcely be brought to a decisive yes or no. When my judgments are merely verbal, but not self-committed, or are hesitant and not decisive, or are those of a detached observer and not oriented toward action, actions may not follow from them. The drive to question leads me to make the connections between these stages of awareness. It drives me to seek new ranges of experience; it puts pressure on, and sometimes explodes, the images by which I try to arrange and contain my experience; it raises questions about the meaning of and connections between my images; it raises further questions about the adequacy of my understanding of such meanings and connections; it suggests, after I have made a judgment: "Well, what are you going to do about it?"

My critics—and in my critical moments, I myself—raise questions about the deficiencies of my experiences, images, conceptions, judgments, and actions. It is the drive to question that propels them, and me, to expand the range of each of these stages of awareness. Such expansion is, in principle, unlimited. There is no point at which, unless our nerve fails, we wish to say: "No more experience, fantasy, understanding, judgment, action."

The unique character of our drive to question, however, is its ability to double back upon itself. By means of it, I question all the states of awareness of which I am capable, their operations, sequences, and relations. There is nothing in me that I cannot question. Every form that the drive to question assumes is subject to questioning. Every operation of the drive to question is subject to review and revision. It is, as it were, in facing itself—in emptying itself—that the drive to question faces the void.

The drive to question is a fundamental tendency and vital force of the human personality. It is not merely in the head. It is in the limbs, in the genitals, in the heart, in the passions, in the darkest and most sensitive recesses of instinct and sensibility. The questions that a man raises are not always conceptual or verbal. "Raising a question" is not only a matter of uttering an interrogative sentence, but more often a matter of attentive experience, alertness, noticing: having an open and hungering attitude toward experience. Questions often take the form of directing attention in a new way, of allowing fresh elements of experience into consciousness, of permitting the preconscious play of affects and images to subvert our ordinary, conventional, conscious sense of reality.[28]

The drive to question arises prior to the verbal, conceptual level; it allows the human animal to alter the stimuli that come to him in his experience as well as to alter his own response to such stimuli.[29] It is a drive that liberates the human animal from the necessity of perceiving, imagining, or conceiving the world or himself in one way only. It is a drive that allows the human animal to keep altering his views of world and self—to invent new formations of world and self, to direct his own evolution.[30] It is, finally, the drive that leads the human animal to feel what no other animals do, namely, anxiety. The components of this anxiety are feelings of helplessness and loneliness;[31] its terminus is the perception of one's own death.[32] For by his endless drive to question a man sooner or later may perceive that all the supports offered by his culture, his social position, and his achievemnts do not remove the fundamental law of consciousness: he stands alone in a darkness and he must die.

Granted that I must die, how shall I live? That is the fundamental human question, which fundamental myths aim to answer.[33] The drive to question allows the human animal to lift his eyes from the sequence of daily routines to perceive the law of his own death, and to struggle for ways of life that assuage death's bitterness. Thus, from the earliest moments of life until death extinguishes it, the drive to question is the principle of human development. It changes its form in each of life's cycles and furnishes the momentum that leads from one stage to the next: from the first sensual exploration, through the building of ideals and ideologies, to wisdom in the face of death.[34] As the human organism that develops through these life stages is one, so also is the drive to question one. Spirit is inquiry.

To divide man into body and mind is, clearly, an error.[35] The drive to question is present or prefigured at every threshold in the development of man. Thus it is important to keep emphasizing that the drive to question is not present only in scientists and students, or shown only in the attainment of clear concepts and well-founded theories. It is a drive that, like any other, may be more or less successfully blunted, stunted, evaded, or blocked, but of itself it keeps working toward its own liberation. Closed minds and fanatical believers are not entirely rare; conventional and imperceptive spirits are legion. Genuinely open, discerning, critical, developing spirits are not a commonplace. But the human psyche is tangled and complex; were more persons taught to allow their attention to illuminate the more remote, tacit, less easily retrievable streams of their own consciousness, they would find in themselves fresh sources of enrichment.[36] Lawrence Kubie writes:

There is abundant experimental and clinical evidence to indicate that traditional conceptions of how human beings think and learn have started from a natural but totally misleading assumption *that we think and learn consciously.* This is not true. Conscious processes are important not for thinking but for sampling, checking and correcting, and as tools for communication. The intake of factual data about the world around us is overwhelmingly preconscious, i.e., *subliminal.* This preconscious input consists of an incessant subliminal bombardment, which goes on both when we are awake and when we are asleep. . . .

Second, the bits of information which are furnished to us this way, whether subliminal or conscious, are then processed . . . on a subliminal level. All of this is just another way of saying that most, if not all, of our thinking is preconscious rather than conscious. Here again, the conscious component is only a weighted and fragmentary sample of the continuous stream of preconscious processing of data. . . .

It is clear that what remains cannot be a true representation of the external world, or of what we are trying to learn, or what is processed internally in the learning process, or of what we "create" by recombining units into new patterns. I once put it that unwillingly we distort what we perceive, and then learn what we have distorted. Psychologists, psychiatrists, neurologists, neurophysiologists have erred together in their undue emphasis on the conscious components of mentation. This has misled the educator into neglecting the *preconscious* instruments of recording, processing and of creating.[37]

But man is not only a question-asker, he is also a symbol-maker. His symbols are the poor tools by which he breaks down the flood of experience, selecting and distorting even as they make it manageable. Thus there is a powerful tension in man between his nostalgia for order and clarity—represented by the world of symbols and institutions—and his limitless drive to raise further questions. Integration and differentiation succeed one another in cycles of development; orderliness gives way to creative ferment.

Yet of the two drives, the drive to question seems prior to the drive to symbolize. It is prior in the sense that when the theoretical systems, symbols, and myths by which we perceive and explain the world prove to be inadequate, the drive to question is the agency both of their embarrassment and their replacement. The drive to question precipitates the disruption of symbol systems in two ways: it directs attention to new experience, in unknown and often threatening areas, and it directs attention to distortions, contradictions, and limitations in our perceptions and our theories.

Thus, by virtue of the drive to question, man is limitlessly open to further revision of his scheme of things. On the one hand, this unbounded openness is the principle of human evolution. On the other, this same openness is the principle of the vertigo and sense of emptiness that accompany the experience of nothingness. The recognition that the drive to question is prior to all concepts, theories, symbols, and myths, and that these latter are merely its tentative and swiftly obsolescent tools, leaves the human animal without the support and solidity to which acceptance of his culture's sense of reality had accustomed him. The structures, values, and aims that his culture had put into existence for him he now pulls back. He can undercut his culture's sense of reality at every point. When the sense of reality is pulled out, he is left swimming in the night air.

In the United States, the openness of the drive to question is cherished as the principle of progress; that it is also the source of the experience of nothingness is silently ignored. Politicians protecting the "free" world, industrialists building a better world through chemistry, scientists seeing themselves as the vanguard of evolution, professors educating young persons for a better tomorrow—all have reason to resist the notion that progress is a self-deception masking self-destruction, that man's tools have become more dangerous to man than the natural environment ever was, and that the human species is not the goal of earth's evolution but only a brief, passing stage en route to something else. The myth of progress through the technical solution of problems does not adequately express the human situation. It is shallow, one-dimensional, repressive, and destructive. But when one loses faith in it, where can one turn?

4. Honesty and Freedom

The experience of nothingness has its source in the drive to question. A valid ethic must be built upon that source. When the experience of nothingness first arose in recent history, it seemed to many that honesty and dishonesty, cruelty and gentleness, and creativity and destruction were of equal value, for nothing at all was of any value. It made as much sense to murder an old man as to tip one's hat to him; either act was of ethical indifference. Camus's Meursault could not care whether his mother died; and he was too indifferent, actually, to pull the trigger in the fight on the beach; his own execution was also a matter of indifference to him.[38] Meursault stood outside the normal values and conventions; in the bright, glaring light of Oran, everything was questionable. But the feeling of indifference arose prematurely. Neither Camus nor Sartre nor other writers about nothingness could maintain their pose of indifference throughout the Nazi period. The reason was twofold.

In the first place, Hitler and Mussolini were self-confessed nihilists, not merely of a literary sort. They had the power to mold human bodies and spirits to their whims. Their crematory ovens greyed the sky of Europe. For many months even after the collapse of France, Camus remained aloof from the struggle until a young friend of his was shot by the Gestapo. Then he concluded that *there are nihilisms that cannot be tolerated*, and at the risk of his own life he joined the underground. In *The Myth of Sisyphus*, *The Plague*, and *The Rebel*, he worked out arguments within the context of the experience of nothingness in order to deny the validity of suicide[39] and murder,[40] and in order to affirm the community of human suffering.[41] Similarly, Sartre was pressed into distinguishing authenticity from inauthenticity, genuine freedom from bad faith, and existentialism from nihilism.[42] Amid the lies of Nazi propaganda, Sartre and his friends longed for honesty like men gasping for necessary air.[43] In brief, Hitler forced men to distinguish between the experience of nothingness, which is human and valid, and nihilism, which draws from that experience corrupting, inhumane, and indefensible conclusions.

In the second place, however, the same human being who experiences nothingness can also reflect upon those capacities of his that make his experience possible. One of the great gifts of Christianity to mankind, Nietzsche wrote, was to teach men to cherish honesty, even if that honesty would later subvert Christianity itself.[44] The source of the experience of nothingness is the drive to question, the drive of honesty, one of whose modalities is that *nostalgie* of which Camus wrote,[45] another the authenticity so important to Sartre.[46] If one reflects upon the exigencies of the drive to question that generate the experience of nothingness, one discovers among them the elements of a very powerful morality. In particular, one is led to reflect upon honesty, freedom, courage, and community.

Honesty, first, leads us to see that the myths and institutions that have shaped our identity are not necessary, solid, and permanent. And at first we are led to feel: "What's the use? Everything is relative. Nothing makes any difference." Then honesty compels another admission: that the ethical relativism in which we find ourselves is not an absolute. It is simply a fact. Just as first we discovered, through the drive to question, that values are relative, so now we discover through the same drive the relativity of relativity. The fact that values are relative to one's culture, time, person, and purpose does not *oblige* us to be ethically indifferent;

a mere fact is not normative. Relativity describes a state of affairs. It is not an excuse but a starting point. *Granted that values are relative, how do I wish to live?* The ethical issue becomes a question of invention and creativity rather than a problem of obedience and obligation.

The experience of nothingness is at first ethically confusing, if one has been nourished by the myth of tradition, the rationalistic myth, or the humanistic myth. The myth of tradition teaches us that wise men in the past knew best, that society knows best, and that the myths and institutions of our culture are not to be questioned. The rationalistic myth teaches us that there is some rational foundation in ethics, some rational and a priori (Kant), or else compellingly emotive (Hume) base that furnishes the axioms by which we judge the complex individual acts we are called upon to perform. The humanistic myth teaches us, despite the indifference with which disease, violence, and death sweep through our ranks, that each human self is unique and valuable. When honesty leads us to see through the inadequacies of such myths as these, it often leaves us yearning just the same. We are disappointed with our fathers, insecure without certainty, depressed by our loss of identity and value.

These three myths are powerful, but they are no longer wholly convincing. The first fails because we cannot consciously take possession of our own identity—come to discover and to invent who we are and wish to be—until the experience of nothingness purges us of our reliance upon our culture; the props must be knocked away if we are to stand on our own. Secondly, a valid ethic does not have its foundations in rational argument but in actual, concrete human actions. When the ethical question arises, men have already been, in Heidegger's word, thrown. They do not begin ethical reflection in a vacuum. By the time they begin ethical reflection, they have already been experiencing, imagining, theorizing, judging, choosing for some time. We do not need to seek some supposedly solid, universal, or eternal base for our actions. We can begin to reflect upon what we, and other concrete historical men, have already been doing.

Thirdly, instead of supposing that humanism depends upon the existence of a unique, valuable, autonomous self, honesty compels us to observe that the human person cannot be wholly distinguished from his physical, cultural, and social environment. The acute self-consciousness of modern Western man is due to exaggerations stemming from the Enlightenment and the Protestant Reformation. Socrates was the first man in history to distinguish himself clearly as an individual, willing to stand over against his community even to the point of death; but even Socrates granted, almost cheerfully, the right of Athens to put him to death. The course of later Western history is often imagined as a progressive heightening of the consciousness of the individual over against the consciousness of the society.

An American walking into a room today—into a cocktail party or a college mixer—imagines himself as an individual among other atomic individuals, and he imagines his problem to be that of "bridging" an enormous gap of silence and distance between himself and others. In many other cultures, men seem to think of themselves primarily as brothers, cousins, kin, or in any case as members in whom group consciousness lives; their problem might be imagined to be, if they so thought of it, how to distinguish themselves from the group at all.

In his famous essay "What is Enlightenment?," Immanuel Kant praised the independent, autonomous individual as the model for a new age in the West.[47] Influential Protestant reformers saw institutions and social groups as the chief sources of corruption, and thought of the conscientious individual, without mediator, as the locus of grace. In both these traditions, society is secondary and possibly corrupting; individual consciousness is the arena of human progress and goodness. Prometheus, alone and defiant against the gods and fates, becomes the modern symbol of the true man.

But perhaps this Western way of imaging the human situation is erroneous. It is possible that there is no such self as westerners have been taught to imagine themselves possessing. Possibly, the self cannot be conceived in a positive way, as some sort of thing inside my body or my personality. The image used by William James may make the maximal claim for the self: it is a sort of *resistance* against culture, society, the world.[48] The self is not some sort of inner object, not some inner, shining permanent core of a man's identity, not the conscious light of analytic reason. I am not a self, never did possess a self, do not have a permanent and indestructible identity, and have no special need to mourn its absence. Certainly, a great many men in human history never imagined that they had (or were) selves, and never felt its lack.[49] Experience may force me to think of myself as a concrete human subject constituted by a series of relations, experiences, perceptions, understandings, judgments, and actions. But images of such subjectivity—like images of God —are fraught with illusion; examined closely, they shatter.

Language betrays us. It makes us talk as if there is an "inner" core of selfhood, over and apart from the "outer" world. The grammatical subject "I" persuades me to imagine an isolated, conscious me over here, previous to interaction with the world over there. Whereas what seems to be the case in fact is that a network of relations to the world is what *constitutes* the self.[50] As the network changes, so does the self. The self has no pure identity, substance, core of its own; it is constituted by activities in engagement with the world. There is no self over and apart from the world. There is only a self *in the world, part of the world, in tension with the world, resistant to the world.* It would be better (although after so many centuries our language scarcely would allow it), to drop the expression "self" entirely, and to speak instead of "a conscious world" or, indeed, "a horizon." I am a conscious world, a horizon, a two-poled organism, a conscious, open-ended, protean, structuring of a world. The world exists through my consciousness and my consciousness through it: not two, but one-in-act.

When I go swimming in the ocean, I do not need to perceive the resistant, tensile waves as foreign to me—outside me, beating against my body, impressing my consciousness through the medium of skin, muscles, and nerves. I can also perceive the ocean as myself; I am it and it is me, in the precise sense that the shock of its resistance shapes my consciousness, while the alertness of my consciousness makes it exist for me. We are not two, but one-in-act. Similarly, in a lecture hall with persons seated next to me, they are not separate, isolated, atomic cores of consciousness, entrapped behind walls of flesh and culturally selected clothes. They are already I, and I am they, in the sense that their presence shapes my consciousness, and the receptiveness of my consciousness allows them to exist for me. We do not have to treat each other like external objects, flashing signals across a chasm. We can address each other as if each of us were already present in the other, as if, like a *thou* to a *thou*, we were a *we*. When you attend to me, you make me exist for you. We can, of course, simply not attend to each other, and thus not exist for one another. A great deal depends on which myth we employ to channel our experience.

In this respect, a peculiar contradiction exists between two myths widely accepted in our culture: the capitalist view that competition is the law of life, and the secular-Christian view that cooperation and community is the law of life. Sometimes these two myths operate side-by-side, as on the editorial page of *The Wall Street Journal.* We alternate between seeing ourselves as rugged individuals, locked in a struggle in which only the fittest survive, in which each man is only for himself and must rely on himself under a dangerous "law of the jungle," and seeing ourselves as backslapping, brotherly, mutually loving "members of a team," engaged in a common project in which our personal interests are subordinated to those of the group in support of the steadily advancing cause of human brotherhood. We celebrate one of these mythologies in justifying our profits by the dangerous risks we have taken, and the other by joining fraternal organizations where it is against the rules to talk business.

A similar contradiction exists, as we have already noted, between the inherent goals of science and technology and the good of concrete, human persons. We try to pretend that every advance of science and technology is by definition a step forward for human beings. But in the eyes of science and technology, concrete human individuals are not persons but units. Similarly, our society puts great stress on intimacy, the personal touch, communication, and unity, but it also teaches persons to be silent about their deepest feelings, fears, terrors, longings, even with those dearest to them. All through our society there are conflicts between our fundamental, unresolved, conflicting myths. If our society seems to be coming apart at the seams, it is because its myths do not cohere.

Then there is freedom. However absurd and confused the myths under whose sway we live, the fundamental fact about our lives is that we choose.[51] We have already been thrown: we are caught in a process in which we have been making choices and in which we must continue to choose. For even not to choose is still a choice. Finding ourselves in the experience of nothingness, we do in fact choose what to do with it. That we choose, inescapably, every moment, is simply a fact. (This fact is not altered by the perception that a great many social, economic, and political choices are made without our participation; to allow them so to be made, all unprotesting, is also a choice). It is also simply a fact that the drive to question is manifest in our behavior.

Suppose, however, that we put the two together: both our radical, inescapable freedom and our drive to question. And suppose that someone then proposes that it is valuable to maximize the number of choices made with understanding and deliberation, and that it is valuable to exercise, strengthen, and to extend the drive to question in every possible way. His argument is that we do, in fact, choose, and the drive to question already operates in us; let us—the proposal runs—make our questions and our choices as full and conscious as possible. "The unexamined life is not worth living." To choose with less consciousness than we might is to allow our choices to be made more by others and by events than by ourselves. To allow our drive to question to languish and grow slack is to cripple the source of personal and social development.

If we accept this argument, we make a great ethical leap. We leap from recognizing the fact of choice and the existence of the drive to question to conferring *value* upon their exercise. Nothing compels us to turn these facts into values. To do so is an act of freedom, a creative act, whose starting place is the experience of nothingness.

There is, however, something fitting about the choice to maximize the consciousness of our choices and to give free rein to the drive to question. Each choice doubles back on itself; both together are mutually reinforcing. To choose to maximize reflective choices is in a peculiar way to be already doing what one is choosing to do, to do it by means of the very operation itself. And to choose to exercise the drive to question is, in a peculiar way, to make reflective choices possible. For it is the drive to question that enables us to gain some poor insight, at least, into the motives, circumstances, conditions, and probable consequences of our choices. We might, of course, choose to blunt the drive to question, to escape or to evade it, and thus to deliver ourselves over to blind compulsions, unrecognized conditioning, and the like. Unless we choose otherwise, the drive to question is easily lost among our other human drives: for security, for status, for pleasure, for evasion. Unless enlightened by probing questions, our choices are more likely than not trapped in patterned responses, anxieties, and inhibitions. Choice and the drive to question require one another.

5. Courage and Community

The third value implicit in the experience of nothingness is courage. The impulse to exercise both the drive to question and conscious choice meets resistance. In the depths of the experience of nothingness, a person often wishes to cry out in despair: "Why bother? Why do anything at all?" And thus at the root of honesty and freedom is an act of sheer creative will, an act of courage. Without courage, honesty is impossible; one avoids painful truths. Without courage, freedom is impossible; one lacks the heart to create. The myth of Genesis, which describes God as the One who begins in darkness and creates light, asserts that man is made in the image of God. Just so, the experience of nothingness places man in the position of *creatio ex nihilo.* For no good reason, from the depths of his own emptiness and abandonment, a man must freely create his own values, his own identity—or fail to do so. Cultural supports, intellectual supports, and emotional supports have been taken away from him; he will be who he will be. In the night the terror of freedom passes through him. He decides for himself whether to seize hold and, if so, which way to bend his life. He reaches into the depths, fingers his bootstraps, and utters "Yes" or "No" out of his own anguish and abandonment.

An account of the requisite courage is given by William James:

Whilst in this state of philosophic pessimism and general depression of spirits about my prospects, I went one evening into a dressing-room in the twilight to procure some article that was there; when suddenly there fell upon me without any warning, just as if it came out of the darkness, a horrible fear of my own existence. Simultaneously there arose in my mind the image of an epileptic patient whom I had seen in the asylum, a black-haired youth with greenish skin, entirely idiotic, who used to sit all day on one of the benches, or rather shelves against the wall, with his knees drawn up against his chin, and the coarse gray undershirt, which was his only garment, drawn over them inclosing his entire figure. He sat there like a sort of sculptured Egyptian cat or Peruvian mummy, moving nothing but his black eyes and looking absolutely non-human. This image and my fear entered into a species of combination with each other. *That shape am I,* I felt, potentially. Nothing that I possess can defend me against that fate, if the hour for it should strike for me as it struck for him. There was such a horror of him, and such a perception of my own merely momentary discrepancy from him, that it was as if something hitherto solid within my breast gave way entirely, and I became a mass of quivering fear. After this the universe was changed for me altogether. I awoke morning after morning with a horrible dread at the pit of my stomach, and with a sense of the insecurity of life that I never knew before, and that I have never felt since. It was like a revelation; and although the immediate feelings passed away, the experience has made me sympathetic with the morbid feelings of others ever since. It gradually faded, but for months I was unable to go out into the dark alone.

In general I dreaded to be left alone. I remember wondering how other people could live, how I myself had ever lived, so unconscious of that pit of insecurity beneath the surface of life. . . .[52]

Images of nothingness, insanity, dread, and insecurity come together.[53] His experience arose from a sudden glimpse "beneath the surface of life." What seems real is not real. The pragmatic, reasonable certainties are symbols by which we keep away the feeling of darkness, and keep ourselves occupied and "sane."

James gives a further account of his long ten-year experience of nothingness. In the pit of his depression he soon faced an overwhelming need—to choose. On February 1, 1870, he wrote:

Today I about touched bottom, and perceive plainly that I must face the choice with open eyes: shall I frankly throw the moral business overboard, as one unsuited to my innate aptitudes, or shall I follow it, and it alone, making everything else merely stuff for it? I will give the latter alternative a fair trial. Who knows but the moral interest may become developed.[54]

And on April 30, 1870, he added:

I think that yesterday was a crisis in my life. I finished the first part of Renouvier's second "Essais" and see no reason why his definition of Free Will—"the sustaining of a thought *because I choose to* when I might have other thoughts"—need be the definition of an illusion. At any rate, I will assume for the present—until next year—that it is no illusion. My first act of free will shall be to believe in free will. . . .

Hitherto, when I have felt like taking a free initiative, like daring to act originally, without carefully waiting for contemplation of the external world to determine all for me, suicide seemed the most manly form to put my daring into; now, I will go a step further with my will, not only act with it, but believe as well; believe in my individual reality and creative power. My belief, to be sure, *can't* be optimistic—but I will posit life (the real, the good) in the self-governing *resistance* of the ego to the world. Life shall [be built in] doing and suffering and creating.[55]

The choice that one makes in the experience of nothingness is not a choice to evade that experience or to mitigate its horror. Such a choice would be a lie. It is important to base one's life upon the experience of nothingness, to continue to return to it, and never to forget it. For the experience of nothingness is a penetrating, truthful experience. It is not an illusion or a threat, but a glimpse into our own reality. The only secure ethical base is the experience of nothingness; any other base is shallow and false. *Granted that I am empty, alone, without guides, direction, will, or obligations, how shall I live?* In the nothingness, one has at last an opportunity to shape one's own identity, to create oneself. The courage to accept despair becomes the courage to be.

The fourth implicit commitment is to community. The Marxist critique of such reflections as these generally asserts that the experience of nothingness is both a private, self-indulgent luxury and a further sign of the decadence of the West. Marxism is an optimistic, activist faith; the experience of nothingness is as much a danger to Marxism as to Western religion and secular liberalism. Moreover, Marxism—like scientific humanism—depends upon "teamwork" and "cooperation." The experience of nothingness may prevent people from giving their whole soul to causes, programs, and slogans, for they recognize that all human institutions and movements are illusory. *Plus ça change, plus c'est la même chose.*

The experience of nothingness liberates persons from conventional institutional demands; it desacralizes the status quo. Thus it is extraordinarily capable of breeding revolutionaries. At first the experience of nothingness collapses distinctions; in its light, one social order seems as bad as another. But the drive to question and to reflective choice, from which the experience of nothingness arises, are powerful criteria for the judgment and the remaking of social institutions. Moreover, utopian revolutionaries have a marked tendency to repeat in bloody form the illusions and myths of the past, whereas the revolutionary who has learned in the night to cherish reflective choice and the drive to question, and to regard institutions as myths, will not expect more of them than they can provide.

In chapter four, I shall speak more fully of the political uses of the experience of nothingness. At present a summary may be useful, and one further implication needs to be drawn. The source of the experience of nothingness is man's inalienable, relentless drive to question. Through fidelity to that drive, a man values choices that are illuminated by the drive to question. Honesty and freedom are, then, his key ethical values. But neither honesty nor freedom are possible except to the person who is unafraid of the truth and unafraid of risks. In order to face the often painful truth and the insecurities of the unknown, a man requires constant, steady courage. Hence, courage is the third key value.

In recent Western traditions, values like honesty, freedom, and courage have been conceived individualistically, as if the autonomous individual were the key analytic unit of ethics. But the work of psychologists and sociologists has shown that ethical values are always social.[56] As Erik Erikson has pointed out, a man could not move out from the lassitude of nothingness unless he shared a "basic trust" in existence, a trust given him as a gift by his parents or by others.[57] Similarly, the drive to question develops socially, and the value of reflective choice is a value highly cherished in some cultures, but not in others. The experience of nothingness arises more frequently in some cultures than in others, and in different forms in each culture. Thus community is the fourth value.

Under the conditions of American culture, however, many persons can put themselves under a series of various cultural and social influences; they can change social class, religion, occupation, nationality, philosophical outlook, personality, behavior, and sets of values. It is becoming increasingly possible in our world for men to live through several profound personal conversions, calling forth in themselves significantly different personalities: a poor Southern

Baptist farm boy can become a wealthy Episcopalian industrialist in New York, abandon everything to become an atheist and a social writer in Brazil, and then live as a Buddhist monk for five years in the Far East. The personality type capable of such alternations has come to be called the "protean personality."[58] The protean personality, it must seem obvious, walks over the experience of nothingness like a man on fragile ice. But the main point for our present purpose is to note the two-sided relation: A man's cultural and social milieu conditions his personality, values, and actions; yet the same man is able, within limits, to choose the milieux whose conditioning will affect him. If you wish to turn a radical into a conservative, involve him in administrative authority; the personality change can be quite profound. For that very reason, however, a person might refuse to enter such a milieu.

In Sartre's phrase, there is never any excuse for man, never; not to choose is also a choice. A man cannot excuse himself by hiding behind his culture, social position, occupation, or the rest. He himself is responsible for remaining loyal to all these—and maybe he should not. The experience of nothingness will teach him how empty all these influences are and offer him leverage against their illusions. Thus the experience of nothingness is, on the one hand, a vaccine against social institutions, and on the other, an achievement dependent upon the contributions of such institutions.

In stable cultures, where roles are clearly defined, individuals do not seem to feel the experience of nothingness (as we do) by way of the confusion, complexity, and mobility of their own experience of cultural forms. They feel some intimation of it, rather, in experiencing the terrors of nature and the gods: in storms, plagues, famines, and the awesome marvels of earth and sky. Their culture as a whole is precarious. Whereas, although our whole culture is also uncertain of its future, the unparalleled pluralism of its internal forms teaches us in new and undercutting ways that no one form is sacred, all are arbitrary.

Without language, without a historical tradition, without travel and leisure for reflection, without the mobility made possible by machines, without the encouragement of honesty and reflective choice, the contemporary experience of nothingness hardly seems conceivable. Other animals do not have it. Under the conditions of American culture today, many men must have it. That is one of the glories of American civilization, and one of the most hopeful signs for the future.

3

Inventing the Self

In order to arrive at having pleasure in everything,
Desire to have pleasure in nothing.
In order to arrive at possessing everything,
Desire to possess nothing.
In order to arrive at being everything,
Desire to be nothing.

In order to arrive at that which thou knowest not,
Thou must go by a way that thou knowest not . . .

In order to arrive at that which thou art not,
Thou must go through that which thou art not.[1]

The experience of nothingness is not new to the human race. I would like to pause briefly to connect the themes we have been discussing to ancient traditions.

1. Action Is Dramatic

I need not be afraid of the void. The void is part of my person. I need to enter consciously into it. To try to escape from it is to try to live a lie. It is also to cease to be. My acceptance of despair and emptiness constitutes my being; to have the courage to accept despair is to be.[2] The void is full of danger; insanity, destructiveness, rage, sadism, and other terrors haunt me. My fears of myself derive, in part, from my culture's fear of itself. Western culture is probably the most violent and heedless of life among all world cultures.[3] Since the age of Reason we have created a new institution: the insane asylum. Insane persons cannot be tolerated in a society of reason, possibly because the insanity in each of us cannot be confessed.[4]

Freedom and risk are coterminous. Rather than face the real and terrifying risks of becoming, many human beings prefer not to develop beyond the structures, rules, and patterns that society gives them. In our society in particular, young people do not dare speak about many of the tensions, impulses, desires, and terrors of their inner life. To reveal their "underground life" would be to appear to others—and even to themselves—a trifle mad. Kubie writes:

The child [has] the right to know what he feels. . . . [T]his will require a new mores for our schools, one which will enable young people from early years to understand and feel and put into words all the hidden things which go on inside of them, thus ending the conspiracy of silence with which the development of the child is now distorted both at home and at school. If the conspiracy of silence is to be replaced . . . children must be encouraged and helped to attend to their forbidden thoughts, and to put them into words, i.e., to talk out loud about love and hate and jealousy and fear, about what goes in and what comes out; about what happens inside and what happens outside; about their dim and confused feelings about sex itself; about the strained and stressful relationships within families, which are transplanted into schools. . . .[5]

The testimony of nihilists since Nietzsche and Dostoevsky has been extremely important. It ruptures the conspiracy and frees us to enter the void inside us. Being is the discovery and acceptance of ourselves as we are: unstructured, formless, free. The path to being lies through the experience of nothingness.

Many persons will not enter the path to being, however, because they instinctively draw back from the experience of nothingness. Instead of truthful consciousness, they prefer the borrowed pretenses of shape, form, structures, rules, roles, and institutions. They give themselves over completely to what their culture accepts as real; that is, they allow the myths of their culture to shape their lives.

In particular, men who speak for an older order (one thinks of William Buckley, Max Rafferty, Ronald Reagan) seem to believe that the primary ethical difficulty today is to find the discipline, will-power, and self-control to obey laws that are already clear. For them, an act is ethical precisely insofar as it falls under a general rule; an ethical action is an exemplification of a universal natural law. It is its universality, its generality, that gives it its ethical weight.[6] By contrast, many persons today—especially young people—find that the primary ethical difficulty is not that of discipline, obedience, or self-control. The difficult task today is to discover which, among conflicting laws, are valid, or to discover laws not yet known but more adequate to the human condition today. In a word, the difficulty is to discover *what* one ought to do. Some young persons feel very keenly that they have the requisite desire, courage, and energy to do what they ought to do, if only they knew what it was. In their eyes, an act is not moral just because it is an instance of a general rule or even a universal. An act is moral only if it is a precisely appropriate response to the many demands of concrete circumstances. It is not generality or universality that gives an action its ethical weight, but *precise and complete appropriateness.* Here, too, at least at first, fidelity to the drive to question seems to leave one structureless, formless, and terrifyingly free. For without rules how do I know what is appropriate?

The primal formlessness of the drive to understand leads to the experience of the void. But the capacity of my drive to question every one of its operations creates for me an ideal of authenticity and honesty. For that capacity implies that every part of myself and my every action falls under judgment. It is impossible, of course, to bring myself wholly under judgment at any one time. I am already a complicated, polymorphous creature long before I gain any capacity whatever to judge myself. My whole world lives in me, shaping me, and I am commixed with that world. My glimpses of my own motives, my own strategies, my own actions are always only piecemeal and partial. Each insight into such matters alters them. To see my self truly at a given moment is thereby to become a different self from the one I was at the immediately preceding moment. (This shifting consciousness is the root of Sartre's conception of *mauvaise foi.*[7]) I am never totally luminous to myself.

Consequently, I know that honesty occurs not by some blazing total act of honesty, but by those small discernments that reveal to me one by one my own deceptions, rationalizations, and merely conformist patterns of behavior. I learn the possibilities of ethical action not through intuition into some transcendental or abstract realm, but through reflection upon my own actual, concrete behavior and that of other men. Action precedes reflection. Men are already acting and have been acting for centuries, and I have been acting for years before I begin to reflect on who I am and who I choose to become.

Twenty-four centuries ago, Aristotle carried out his ethical task from a comparable starting point. He came to his mature ethical vision near the end of his life, after having been steeped in the glimpses into the abyss provided by Greek tragedy,[8] and after long reflection on the idiosyncrasies and contingencies that characterize the actual, concrete activities of men.[9] When he began to give the lectures that students transcribed as the *Nicomachean Ethics*, the dominant view of the subject was as Plato had earlier set it forth: the good is an ideal form, eternal and unchanging, and in this world of shadows good men try to discern it, to meditate upon it, to imitate it, and to participate in it.[10] In his earlier work, Aristotle had also thought of the good as a fixed and complete form, to be contemplated and yearned for. But as the years went on, Aristotle came to be convinced that a new and more supple approach to ethics was required.[11] I find five cornerstones in his later thinking.

i. The subject matter of ethics is the actual, concrete practice of men. Ethical reflection is not primarily an analysis of ideal forms, general laws, universal principles, logical connections, or conceptual and linguistic puzzles, but a dialectical critique of concrete actions.[12] The subject matter of ethics is not *man*—abstract, universal, under general laws—but *concrete men acting*. The subject matter is not "the objective order of good," but the acts of concrete human subjects.[13]

2. The happiness that all men claim to seek is not to be conceived of as a psychological state of contentment, an excess of pleasure over pain, an inner equilibrium or peace, a sense of satisfaction, a comfortable middle-of-the-road avoidance of conflict and disorder.[14] On the contrary, happiness (*eudaimonia*) is *activity;* it is *to act* to the fullest of one's capacities.[15] In Aristotle's view action comes first. The feeling of pleasure or satisfaction is secondary, a sort of overflow that may or may not be present.[16] To be happy is not to do little, to be passive, to be content; it is to act, and to act well. Indeed, *eudaimonia* is to be translated as well acting.[17]

3. The criterion of acting well, moreover, is not a set of general laws, a universal, an objective order, a transcendental, but the example of certain concrete human beings whose names can even be mentioned—men like Pericles.[18] Just as the subject matter of ethics is concrete human action, so the criterion for discriminating between acting well and acting poorly is the example of specifiable concrete human beings. To be sure, theoretical reasons can be given in support of the choice of these models rather than others. We shall return to this point.

4. Concrete human models like Pericles are chosen as the criterion for acting well, not so that other men can imitate the content of their actions, but so that men can learn the process of acting well. Aristotle is firmly committed to the view that each individual agent is unique,[19] and that each situation in which action is called for differs from every other.[20] Hence, it would not make sense for other men to try to be like Pericles in the sense of doing what Pericles did, but only in the sense of meeting ethical decisions in their life in the way that Pericles met such decisions in his. One need not repeat Pericles, like a carbon copy. But, by reflection upon the actions of Pericles, one may well discern a dynamic structure in the procedures by which Pericles shaped his life that will be helpful in

building up a corresponding structure in one's own life.

Kenneth Burke remarks in a brilliantly perceptive study of action that Aristotle's conception of act is a dramatic conception.[21] For Aristotle, life is energy-in-act, and a work of art succeeds insofar as it re-creates living processes. The essence of tragedy is action.[22] Moreover, art is the heuristic framework through which Aristotle approaches ethics. Ethical reflection is not an examination of rules, laws, imperatives, or obligations; it is the study of an art. The artist and the athlete provide Aristotle's central metaphors for ethical achievement. By contrast, philosophers since the Enlightenment tend to use the conceptual framework of logic and law-like behavior based on sciences like geometry (Spinoza), mechanics (utilitarianism), and biology (American naturalism). They do not understand that action is dramatic. Yet every human life tells a story, and, beyond that, the culture itself is shaped by stories. Culture is a field of nature, as biology is.[23] What makes culture different from nature is identical with the emergence of ethics: man shapes himself by his stories. Man is the only species whose future is not biologically determined.

5. The dynamic structure that leads to acting well has two sources, one outside our control and the other within it. Outside our control, at least initially, is the way we have been shaped by our culture and our environment to feel and to perceive in certain ways. Aristotle insists upon this point frequently; without a certain kind of upbringing, acting well (as Pericles did) is so unlikely as to be nearly impossible.[24] If we feel shame and pride, pleasure and pain, in undisciplined, untutored ways, we shall not value self-criticism, inquiry, honesty, courage, or other qualities indispensable for ethical development.[25] In ethical as in physical development, Aristotle recognizes the incidence of a certain lameness and blindness.[26]

One source of the structure of acting well comes to us, then, as a gift.[27] The other source is our own responsibility, for it concerns which of our human capacities we choose to value by making it (or them) central to our actions. Such choices have consequences, and to choose well here is to have won more than half the battle,[28] whereas to choose badly is to involve ourselves in future confusions and contradictions.

One can discern in Aristotle's treatment of the capacities that men like Pericles choose to develop a sequence of operations. Certain operations of *experiencing and feeling* are a first prerequisite.[29] Acuity in *perceiving* the point of complex ethical situations, acuity in hitting the mark, is the pivotal capacity.[30] The *judgment* that one has truly hit the mark, that is, the ability to discriminate between alternative views of what in fact constitutes the mark, is a further prerequisite. For everyone has some view or other of the situation, but the heart of the matter is singularly difficult to hit, while the number of ways by which one can miss it are nearly infinite.[31] Less clearly developed in the Aristotelian analysis is the factor of *desire, willingness, decisiveness;*[32] for unless one has the will to act well, not all the insight or good judgment in the world leads to actual acts.[33]

In brief, Aristotle discerns a sequence of basic human operations, the absence of any one of which vitiates good action. That sequence forms a powerful, concrete, operable structure. By defining the operational *structure* Aristotle is spared the necessity of defining the *content* of ethical behavior. Thus his ethical system offers considerable concrete guidance while refusing to state which acts are good, to insist upon universal commandments, or to specify a code. Each ethical agent is left with the freedom and responsibility for shaping the content of his own horizon: shaping himself and his world, shaping his worldself.

For Aristotle, as for the Greeks generally, one of the foremost categories of ethical thinking is that of conversion, a conversion achieved through dialectical reflection.[34] To become a lover of wisdom is to change one's way of life, not merely to change one's opinions. Thus dialectic is not so much the search for contradictions or inconsistencies in our ethical language. It is an inquiry: (a) into how adequately our actions achieve what our words say we seek, (b) into whether we actually do what we say we do, and (c) into how serious we are about bringing the many elements of our lives into a fundamental integrity of consciousness, word, and act. The life not worth living, Aristotle learned from his tutor, is the unexamined life. It is not the mind merely that must be examined, but the life. Otherwise, if the study of ethics does not lead to acting well, what is its point?

2. Decision Lies with Discernment

We have seen that for many persons today the problem is not how to find the will to follow a clearly known directive of conscience; the problem is how to perceive what to do at all. In the much more stable society of fourth-century (B.C.) Athens, Aristotle's concerns were not the same as ours. But when he singles out the importance of ethical discernment ($\alpha\check{\iota}\sigma\theta\eta\sigma\iota\varsigma$), and stresses the difficulties in developing it, he singles out precisely the phenomena we are struggling with.[35]

Aristotle did not think of ethics in terms of duty. The metaphors in his writings are not derived from the figure of a commanding God, from codes of legal observance, or even from obedience to the internalized strictures of one's father. The metaphors are taken almost entirely from art and athletics. Aristotle recognized that most men are not, in fact, to be much praised for their moral behavior; without feeling guilty, most prefer money, pleasure, or unquestioning conformity to moral achievement. But there lie in moral excellence such grace and such beauty that some men, at least, are seduced by them as athletes are, as artists are.

For Aristotle, ethics is a matter of inspiration, desire, and arduous seeking; it is not a matter of "Do your duty." On the other hand, men of grace and beauty are models by which to measure oneself and to be measured; ethics is not a matter of "Do what you please." Morality is a matter of acting with grace and beauty, because one is drawn to—chooses to be drawn to—grace and beauty.

Like Aristotle, we are not moved by appeals to "obligation" or "duty." The Protestant ethic and the Kantian approach to morality, which had never affected Aristotle, no longer comfort us. We, too, are relatively confident in our own good will, in our own ardent desire for moral excellence; no one has to push us—we desire to be honest and effective in action. Our greatest ethical perplexity is how to discover a method for discerning what to do in any given situation. We do not want rules. We want to learn discernment.

That is precisely what Aristotle made central in his discussions, only he pointed out that, much as he would like to teach it, discernment can't be taught.[36] A father cannot pass discernment on to his son; a teacher cannot pound it into his students. Sons and students must develop it on their own. It is the root of their freedom and their identity. You can propagandize an ideology; you cannot mass-produce the discernment that makes liberty possible.

On the other hand, you can help to establish the conditions that make the emergence of discernment more probable and more frequent. That is the most a philosopher (or a parent, or a citizen) can do. You can lead a man to liberty; he himself must drink. Thus discernment is taught by a sort of indirection. It is approached by way of negatives. "The truth is not x, not y, not z; look over here, then; not a, not b, not c; once more now, not m, not n, not o." The bright and willing man begins to catch on; the dull or the unwilling never see. Discernment makes the difference.[37] But in order to sensitize persons to that critical point, it is necessary to seduce their attention away from rules and regulations, laws and structures, general principles and directives. They must be led to discern that the critical point is discernment.

The question to which discernment provides the basis of an answer runs as follows. How can one make concrete ethical decisions sensitively and intelligently when each concrete situation and each ethical agent are different from every other? Living as we are in a stream of contingent, irreversible, and unrepeatable events, there are several ways in which we might imagine our ethical task. Do we learn from our past by formulating principles drawn from experience? Do certain natural laws (or institutional structures) direct us, as they direct the behavior of gases and stars (or encourage routines and bureaucratic patterns)? Should we try to respond to each situation afresh, with honesty and sincerity—or, perhaps, love—as our only guides?

In my reading in the history of philosophy, one text more than any other has offered me a way to cast light on the problem of concrete ethical decisions. I want to comment on that text with precision and in detail, in order to bring its light to bear upon our own perplexities. The text comes from Aristotle's *Nicomachean Ethics*, Book II, chapter vi. It is the fruit of the long argument of the preceding chapters, and presents in a single, complicated sentence Aristotle's conception of "wisdom in action" (*phronesis*).[38] Aristotle is not concerned with what makes an ethical theory correct, but with what makes a man's singular, concrete actions good. We shall have to unpack each of his phrases one by one. The text in question runs:

Error is multiform . . . , whereas success is possible in one way only (which is why it is easy to fail and difficult to succeed—easy to miss the target and difficult to hit it); . . .
Moral excellence, then, is a settled *disposition* determining the
choice of actions and emotions,
hitting the right measure *for us*,
according to our principle (*logos*)
of *acting*
exactly as the wise man (*phronimos*) would act.[39]

There is a second text that supports the first. It emphasizes Aristotle's insistence on the relationship of the whole personality to discernment: "As a man is, so do ethical matters appear to him."[40] To the jaundiced eye, even red appears yellow; the determinedly optimistic person refuses to see tragedy and the absurd. Only the authentic, genuine, free person sees—so far as it is given man—truly. The second text runs: "For the good man judges everything correctly; what things truly are, that they seem to him to be . . . what chiefly distinguishes the good man is that he sees the truth in each kind, being *himself* as it were the standard and the measure. . . ."[41]

The point made in each of these texts is identical: the standard, the measure, the criterion of ethical action in concrete situations is the judgment of the *phronimos*—of the good, wise man. The standard is not some eternal code written in the stars. Neither is it a code written in the hearts of men. It lies in the fallible, but skillful, developed, and experienced judgment of a certain kind of man.

There is a kind of circularity in Aristotle's argument; Aristotle had as dialectical and playful a mind as any man who ever lived.[42] The circularity consists in saying that the good man acts as the good man would act—the good man is the standard for the good man. Such circularity is beneficent. It forces us to accept what is today easy enough to accept: that if there is to be an ethic at all, it cannot come from eternal codes or from traditions or conventions. It cannot come from others; it must come from men themselves.

But from which men? It cannot come from all men, and possibly not even from a majority. Aristotle writes: "It appears to be pleasure that misleads the mass of mankind; for it seems to them to be a good, though it is not, so they choose what is pleasant as good and shun pain as evil."[43] It is not what pleases anyone that is automatically good, but what would please the good man. Who is this good man who hangs over our head, against whose tastes and instincts we are measured? Who is this model to whose lineaments we must be chopped?

Aristotle genuinely wishes us to be free.[44] He does not define a model whose weight we must carry for all time. He does not establish a list of specifications, which every good man thenceforward must meet. He does not turn his *phronimos* into a set of twenty commandments, or even ten, or five, that must be followed.[45] Aristotle is aware that it is extremely difficult to define how a good man would act, "especially in particular cases."[46] For "different men are inclined by nature to different faults."[47] How would one "define in what manner and with what people and on what set of grounds and for how long one ought to be angry?"[48] And how would one define the point at which this man is no longer gentle but just plain timid, or that man is no longer manly but just a quick-tempered bully?[49]

If Aristotle were to try to write out a set of dos and don'ts for moral excellence, his specifications would necessarily be abstract and general, that is, not precisely suited to each individual and each situation. But he recognizes that each ethical agent is unique. So what would be the point of a list of abstract ethical rules?[50] They would only make people unethical by leading them to miss the entire point. The point is, "The decision lies with discernment."

The *phronimos*—the sensitive and intelligent agent—perceives truly. The easily corrupted man sees badly. How does one go about teaching oneself to see truly? How does one become an authentic, honest, courageous human being? In the end, it is only by such instruction that Aristotle can break the circularity of his argument. Aristotle assumes that most of us are sick. We do not see clearly; we are not free. We learn to be satisfied, in ourselves and others, "with even a tincture of moral excellence."[51] Still, we are responsible for our own health, our own readiness. The guiding metaphor of the *Nicomachean Ethics* is not duty; it is craftsmanship, artistic skill,[52] and—more precisely—athletic excellence.[53] To act well in a complicated situation, as all situations are, is like an archer "to hit the mark exactly."[54] How does one become an expert *phronimos?* How does one develop one's skills as a human being? How does one sharpen one's eye so that it sees truly?

These questions, for Aristotle, are political questions. Ethics is a branch of politics.[55] The reason is a powerful one: the aims, practices, and customs of the state shape the experiences, feelings, and perceptions of individuals within them. The quality of individual life depends to a great extent upon the quality of the institutions and structures of the state. This is not the place to trace the entire ethical-political thought of Aristotle, most of which is now dated or at least too grossly stated to be useful. The point I wish to emphasize is that in the Aristotelian view the ethical problem is a problem of becoming, a problem of development. Ten years from now, what sort of man do I wish to be? What acts must I now choose in order to develop those skills that later will allow me to be strong, spontaneous, reliable, and flexible? Aristotle recommends that one live out the stories of the poet, the sculptor, the craftsman, the Olympic athlete, and make of one's life an art of action.

In Aristotelian ethics, a man must invent his own identity. He tries to discern—from his present impulses, pleasures, pains, instincts, reactions when surprised or afraid, and the like—what are the hidden, inner springs of his own spontaneities. Then he tries to project the future image he would like to act out. Then he begins by his actions to shape the drift, direction, and depth of his personality-to-be. The test of how well he succeeds is based upon how accurately he discerns his own unique possibilities, and how deeply instinctive and spontaneous become his efforts to keep the path of discernment clear. Each man's own starting places (*archai*), proper measure, experiences, feelings, perceptions, and tendencies are peculiar to him and unique. He must perceive himself truly—not all at once, limpidly, but step by step—ferreting out his own self-deceptions. Man is not a truly perceiving animal; he may try to become so.

My interpretation of Aristotle differs from conventional interpretations in two ways.[56] First, I call attention to all those texts in Aristotle's discussion that emphasize the nonrational components of *phronesis.* Once one notices how very many and clear such texts are, it is impossible to call Aristotle a rationalist without feeling how gross and misleading that characterization is. Secondly, I emphasize the constant series of conversions to which Aristotle calls the ethical agent. His is an ethic of self-liberation through honest discernment and reflective action.

On one key point, I need to add, Aristotle misleads most of his interpreters. His ethic of the mean, beginning at Book II, chapter vi, and ending at the end of Book V, chapter xi, has been taken as the heart of his ethic. I think it is a grave mistake so to regard it. Aristotle was, like many thinkers today, enamored of mathematical models, and he thought he perceived in the theory of the mean a useful device for illustrating the range of opposite patterns of behavior through which the ethical agent has to make his way, as if between Scylla and Charybdis. His aim seems to have been to shed some light on one of the points in his definition of what constitutes the good man, in the chief text given above—the point about "choosing the mean relative to us." Yet Aristotle's ultimate conclusion is that his mean is different for each agent, and can be arrived at only through discernment. Hence, his attempt to systematize his view of the dispositions that made discernment frequent, easy, and pleasurable—the image of the mean—has the countereffect of taking our attention away from discernment.

On the one hand, his account of the virtues and vices offers us a descriptive survey of the actual behavior of the Greeks, and in that sense it is enlightening and concrete. On the other hand, the systematic device of the mean, in which each virtue appears as the head of a triangle above[57] two opposed vices, is too artificial, and it gives an impression of ethics as mechanical, calculating, and middle-of-the-road, which Aristotle clearly does not wish to give.[58] One wonders if Aristotle's students didn't like this part of the ethics best because it was easier to follow, remember, and systematize in their notes. In any case, I regard the device of the mean as a wrong alley for Aristotle to have taken, and when Book VI picks up again, the argument about the exact nature of practical wisdom and of the discernment that is its heart resumes the high level of the main argument.

That main argument makes plain that to become a good man is to grow in the courage to discern honestly, and in the courage to act as one discerns. Honesty is on the side of intuitive instincts; courage on the side of desiring instincts. The two are conjoined sides of the one same human being: "Man is desiring intelligence; or intelligent desire."[59] Since Greek society was relatively stable, and since a tragic sense of life was so powerful it hardly needed to be mentioned, Aristotle did not need to write of the experience of nothingness. But if a man must trust to his own discernment, and also must place the constitution of the state under judgment on a par with the constitution of other states (of which Aristotle had already collected 158 examples[60]), then it is apparent today, if not explicitly to Aristotle,[61] that man lives in darkness and chaos. The brilliantly clear sun of the Mediterranean and the rapid advances of Greek science may have made images of order and light seem stronger to Aristotle than to us.[62] The concrete predicament of the man of practical wisdom, no less than that of the man of discernment and courage today, is fragile and tragic. There is a continuity in the human situation, through cultural stability and crisis, rise and decline, that allows men through the ages to hear one another crying out in the night.

3. Three Myths of the Self

A strong Protestant tradition from Northern Europe, many centuries after Aristotle, urges me to base my ethical struggles on the command of God.[63] Even good Englishmen, far removed from Continental schools of divinity, bid me to think of ethics in terms of feelings of obligation and duty.[64] Yet I always feel rise within me a great resistance to anyone who speaks to me of ethics as some form of duty, whether it is a Catholic priest, a Protestant theologian, or a Kantian philosopher. The resistance reaches a highwater mark when I read Kierkegaard's meditation upon Abraham in *Sickness Unto Death.*[65]

I feel an inner release, a sense of liberation, when I do not think of ethics as duty but as invitation, as invention, as creation, as possibility. And I have been led to spin my own myth to describe ethics. It is the myth of the drive to question.

Let mind and heart imagine, for a moment, a man who struggles to allow the drive to question to unfold and to penetrate into every aspect of his life. That drive leads him quietly and peacefully to probe his own motives, modes of perceiving, actions, and purposes. He is not eager to "analyze" himself; he does not regard himself as a machine. He does not probe himself out of feelings of guilt or anxiety, but just because he loves the light. His drive to question leads him to strive toward a radical singleness in his spontaneities, thoughts, words, and actions. It cuts again and again into the tangled roots of his ineradicable bad faith.

His drive to question, he finds by experience, flourishes best in community. However much his own drive to question prompts him toward accurate discernment, it is most often the attention and questioning of others that unmask his self-deceptions. He cannot bear too much light about himself, since he already hates himself too much, already feels too uncertain and insecure. "The one thing I hate most about marriage," he was once heard to remark, "is the honesty it forces down my throat." It sometimes seems to him that wives are given to husbands (and vice versa) to speak the painful truths one partner could not face alone.

The myth of duty is one dominant way of structuring ethical experience in our culture; the myth of utilitarianism is another. The latter must also be distinguished from the myth I am trying to weave. The utilitarian story, then, envisages a man whose delicately calibrated needs require delicately adjusted satisfactions so that an equilibrium in which pleasure exceeds pain may be maintained. The utilitarian myth is, of course, powerful in a scientific, technological, capitalistic culture; it dominates English and American philosophy. It is easily made amenable to a psychoanalytic theory of successful "adjustment," to a pragmatism that eschews the rash commitments and deeds required to live according to an ideology and, in general, to a safe middle class view of life.[66] Philip Rieff has spoken of this outlook as *The Triumph of the Therapeutic*,[67] although there are, of course, many hardheaded businessmen and political administrators who have scant interest in "therapy." They have a great deal of interest in reducing human tensions, not by meeting problems head-on, but by mastering the mechanisms by which they come to our attention. It is good managerial practice not to argue over substantive issues, but to diagnose a situation functionally and then to isolate and pacify the agents of tension. In dealing with social groups, the utilitarian myth calls for a sort of engineering; in dealing with the self, it calls for a sort of stimulus manipulation. In both cases, the underlying myth imagines man to be a complicated machine, to be understood and controlled functionally.

The myth by which I am trying to seduce as many of you as I can, however, is quite different from the myths of duty and of utilitarianism. Imagine, again, the story of a man born a prisoner—doubly a prisoner, in fact, for he is unaware of his servitude. He has been taught that his servitude is normal, and has even been led to be grateful for it. Then, at one point or another, this man awakens; slowly he begins to recognize the state in which he has been living. Moreover, he recognizes that *he himself, and no one else, has been responsible for that state.* He acquiesced in it; he was satisfied in it; he was grateful for it. And yet now that he sees his former self-deception, he realizes that he could have recognized it long ago. Even then he had the power that he has now: the power to attend, to question, to discern, and to break free. Step by step, he begins to act like a free man, penetrating one self-deception after another, often discouraged by what he discovers about himself, but refusing to quit even when he catches himself in continuing dishonesties. (In the attempt to be honest, are not one's own dishonesties the greatest sorrows?) Thus, never wholly equal to the demands of his relentless drive to question, he learns to fashion small acts of honesty, courage, and freedom.

Morality, according to this myth, is not conceived of as the acquitting of obligations or as the maintenance of a pleasurable equilibrium called happiness. Morality is a slow and painful self-liberation. That self-liberation, moreover, has social and political consequences. It is not solitary but communal. It is aimed at political actions that are free and freedom-serving.

The source of a morality of self-liberation is, I repeat, a concrete drive already evident, however weakly, in the lives of each of us: the drive to question ourselves, a well-founded suspicion concerning our facility in deceiving ourselves and playing roles, a profound dissatisfaction with the scatteredness and unconnectedness of our lives. To shape our ethical perception by the drive to raise questions rather than by the sense of duty is to gain leverage against totems, taboos, and the dark impulses of the will. It is to gain leverage against the calculating safety and narcissism symbolized by sub-urbia and academia, the holy lands of utilitarianism. It is to gain leverage even against the myth about self-liberation. For to base oneself upon the drive to raise questions is to be willing to question the way one presently raises questions; it is to circle ever more profoundly into the depths beneath one's present comprehension. It implies the perception that one's present knowledge is a form of ignorance, a *docta ignorantia*, a foretaste of the void that underlies our consciousness. It raises the questions that both civilization and the individual would prefer to evade. It sees that all those concrete forms and pressures of civilization that are meant to be internalized by the individual are not sacred but limited, more or less arbitrary, and always to be examined and weighed.

Throughout this inquiry, I have tried to make plain that the concrete inescapable drive to raise questions is not a merely ra-tional or intellectual drive. Pick up the writings of recent analytical philosophers of ethics; clearly they do not describe the ethical life as we experience it. They spend far too disproportionate an amount of attention upon words, principles, reasons, logical connections: in a word, upon the mind. Hence I wish to emphasize as strongly as I can that to conceive the meaning of *horizon* correctly one must recognize that a horizon cannot, even in principle, be wholly ex-pressed in words.

The reasons are two. First, a horizon is always undergoing change; to express it is already to have moved to another. Secondly, the subjective pole of a horizon is defined not only by clear under-standings and precise concepts and neatly pragmatic interests, but also by polymorphous experience, fantasies, images, impressions, moods, impulses, and a dark love of the absurd and the irrational (we do so many important things, finally, just for the hell of it). It is also defined by judgments whose satisfaction depends upon the fulfillment of conditions too extensive and numerous to articulate. As the subjective pole of our horizon is complex, so also is the objective pole. We often "feel" that our perceptions are correct or incorrect without immediately being able to articulate the roots of this feeling.[68] Our whole sense of the reality of the world and of ourselves—our worldself—is a human, not only a rational, sense. A horizon cannot be exhaustively stated in words. It can only be adumbrated through the employment of symbols.

4. Truth is Subjectivity

"Symbols," writes Rollo May, "are specific acts or figures . . . while myths develop and elaborate these symbols into a story." The psychological function of symbol and myth is twofold. First, "they are man's way of expressing the quintessence of his experience— his way of seeing his life, his self-image, and his relations to the world of his fellow men and of nature." Secondly, they carry "the *vital meaning* of this experience."[69] In a word, myths are in some not very clearly understood way the bearers of psychic power, life, and energy. They function regressively when they elicit "the repressed, unconscious, archaic urges, longings, dreads and other psychic content." They function *progressively* when they "reveal new goals, new ethical insights and possibilities," when they "are a breaking through of greater meaning which was not present before." "By drawing out inner reality" symbols and myths "enable the person to experience greater reality in the outside world."[70]

Two metaphors hidden in the word "education" express the two characteristics of myth: *e-ducatio*, myths draw out inner reality; *educ-action*, myths are the vital force of action. They express a person's horizon, and they also move him to act.[71]

A man's horizon is always on the move; it changes with action. Myths tell stories precisely because the essence of a story is action, and action defines a future—either this line of development or that other one. A myth, therefore, is dynamic. In a similar way symbols are dynamic. As parts of a myth, they are charged with powers of attraction or repulsion, illumination or depression, expansion or fear.

When an incoming freshman walks across a campus for the first time, or when he receives a white diploma on graduation day, he is living out a story that has been shaping his psyche for a long time. In the United States, a college education is a sacred rite for the elite. Suitable emotions ought to be felt upon entering it and leaving it; thousands of actions, requiring great time, effort, discipline, and planning were directed by that rite. Feelings of awe, expectation, nostalgia, and loss are appropriate at both ends of the rite. "Well-rounded man," "skilled expert," "educated man," "responsible citizen of tomorrow" are the official symbols, but a modest sense of achievement, a feeling of growing poise, increasing sexual maturity, and "one more step out of the way" are corresponding private symbols.

A diploma is not the same as a transcript of grades; long after the latter has been forgotten, the former will be meaningful. The symbols and myths of military service, of academic life, of the business world, of politics, and of the Peace Corps also charge our actions. So do ideologies like private enterprise, social reform, socialism; political orientations like liberal and conservative; class preferences regarding smells, colors, shapes, manners; personal attitudes toward mothering, being mothered, emotional independence, a man shedding tears, competition, loving; religious affirmations or denials like atheism, fundamentalism, liberal belief, mysticism, and the like. Symbols such as these define horizons. Accordingly, men perceive, imagine, understand, and act in the world in endlessly varied ways.

A theory of education that did not attend to differences in horizon would not be sensitive to the springs of perception and understanding. Most of the worthwhile arguments in a man's lifetime involve a mutual exploration of horizons. The heart of learning what it is to be a man is to learn empathy for the multiplicity of horizons in human history. A good teacher focuses on the horizon of each student, not for purposes of therapy or of an encounter for its own sake, but in order that both together may focus on the subject matter.

The point is that direct access to reality or to ideas is not possible.

All known reality is known by and through human subjects; it is part of a human horizon. Men come to an issue from different directions, with different expectations; that is why the transmittal of knowledge is such a delicate task, and why the temptation to appeal to "objectivity" is so strong. If only we could eliminate subjectivity entirely! If only men could approximate learning machines! How quickly, then, information could be transmitted. Education through the personal appropriation and expansion of one's own horizon is much more messy, complex, and obscure, involving as it does fantasy and feeling, partial insights and beloved obscurities, resistances and longings, ambitions and inhibitions, social reinforcements and private terrors.

Education through subjectivity is as different from education through objectivity as symbols are from signs. The American flag, for example, is not merely a geographical signpost: "Here begin the territorial boundaries of the United States." It does not merely point to some object, as literally and as single-mindedly as possible. It is a symbol. That is to say, it includes a reference to human subjects in their subjectivity. It speaks of their history and their aspirations, their experience and their theories. In that way it expresses a horizon: a national (if one may so speak) worldself, an identity, a way of perceiving and of proceeding. There is no creed that exhausts what is included in being an American; there is no single set of propositions, to be understood in a single, fixed way, in which all and only Americans believe. There is no one clear concept, or even a broad pragmatic consensus, that one must confess in order to count as an American.

Similarly, the individual person is not merely designated by his proper name; a proper name is not like a number. That name has a history to it, a story (or perhaps a nonstory, since every story suppresses enormous detail); a person's name is a symbol. Again, a person does not commonly make important decisions in such a way that all the motives, reasons, and elements of that decision are clear, conscious, and expressible; quite the contrary. You smile when a friend tries to enumerate for you all the reasons why he has decided he wants to marry the girl he is going with; the reasons he states frequently have little to do with his choice.

Again, two persons who seem to share similar convictions, creeds, and pragmatic ways of operating may engage in a common action and, nevertheless, derive enormously different significance from it.[72] How many other persons besides Truman Capote read in the *New York Times* the short five-line account of a murder in Kansas? Roommates will attend a course or hear a lecture; one is extremely moved, enough to change his life, while the other is untouched. When we are asked to describe someone or to write a letter of recommendation, the few poor words we have at our disposal scarcely hint at thousands of subtle distinctions: "John is a well-mannered young man, bright, dependable, etc." Think how many millions of boys such adjectives fit; think how many Boy Scouts there are.

Who are you? What do you wish to be? To answer those questions you must tell a story. The more you tell that story, particularly if a psychiatrist, for example, monitors your narrative, the more often the shape of that story will begin to shift. You will find scores of stories you might tell. Which one is true? Which story represents the real you? Possibly none of them. Or all. We are in the same situation regarding myths about ourselves as we are regarding myths about the world, and for the same reason. All such myths are subject to questioning. From a different point of view, given different presuppositions, in a different perceptual framework, the same "facts" lose their solidity; other narratives become plausible; earlier versions will not do at all. Our lives fall apart; we make them and remake them like images in a kaleidoscope. Thus it is, perhaps, that wise men of the East find the myth of the ego—the myth of solid personal identity continuous over time—the most illusory myth of all. As there is no objective version of the world, so also there is no objective version of the self. "No man judges me; neither do I judge myself," St. Paul says, "The Lord alone judges."[73] Short of the Lord, we are uncertain about our identity or the character of our action.

Yet we do have an identity and we do act. The self-image through which we act is, of course, a myth. It is the story we tell ourselves about ourselves, or (quite possibly) the story that our speech evades but our actions reveal. Action cannot take place except through form; action is the structuring of our present and future relations. Action is always part of a story, and hence part of a myth. Even a tale told by an idiot, signifying nothing, will hold us spellbound precisely because its randomness is counterpoint to our expectation of form. As a musician plays with our sense of time—at times holding back, at times surprising by anticipation—so does every myth relate to structures against which it plays its own counterpoint.[74]

Action without myth is logically impossible. A man's life does not live out a code, a creed, or a logical set of principles; a life tells a story. If modern lives seem routine and storyless, isn't it because so many persons are content to drift? Many seem so thoroughly shaped by the institutions, political parties, and social classes to which they belong that one never hears them speak in their own voice; they are mouthpieces for what others expect of them. Their myth is exhausted by the myths of the collectives to which they belong. They are shells without a center, human beings in appearance only, men and women empty of a story of their own.

Elementary health and morality (according to the myth by which I am trying to seduce you) are measured by a person's achievement in raising questions about the myths into which he was born, weighing them and sifting them, until the myths by which he lives have been chosen by himself. But *excellence* in health and morality are measured by a choice of myths that maximize personal and communal development in these four values: honesty, courage, freedom, and the ability to value other persons for themselves.

What is inherently valuable about the myth I am proposing? It does not impose itself upon us with binding necessity; most human beings in history have not been, it seems, conspicuously attached to it. There are not, as Pascal was fond of saying, three honest men in a century. The advantage of the myth of raising questions and of discovering-inventing one's own myths is that one chooses thereby a myth that does not hide its face either from the void or from the conditions of concrete action.

Secondly, it is a myth that encourages its own constant revision, one's own conversion, deepening, and development. One can, according to this myth, change one's present conception of oneself profoundly and still be faithful to the basic myth. For the basic myth does not insist that in our present frame of mind we have already raised the relevant, critical questions or made the most fundamental choices, but only that we are pledged to doing so, once we see how such steps are to be taken.

Thirdly, the myth I am proposing—the myth of self-liberation and self-appropriation—recognizes that the self is not an atomic particle but a worldself, a thou, whose development is interdependent with the development of other human beings in the same qualities to which it aspires for itself.

Finally, it is a myth whose consequences for human institutions are radical rather than liberal, revolutionary rather than reformist, unafraid of violence but chastened by the self-defeating consequences of violent revolutions in recent history.

So far we have said too little about the social and institutional implications of the myth I am proposing. Ethics, Aristotle has taught us, is a branch of politics. The same cultural symbols that are major and indispensable sources of political power are also among the sources shaping all ethical actions. If discernment is the decisive point in Aristotle's "wisdom in action," those cultural myths that in America shape our patterns of discernment must be examined next.

4

Myths and Institutions

The managers of institutions like to think that they are realistic, pragmatic, unflappable men: think of the White House staff under Kennedy and under Nixon. They speak in clipped voices when questioned about disaster. "Difficulties don't swamp us," their silent gray eyes assure us. "One event cancels out another. No panic here."

Institutional men like to think that institutions are pragmatic agencies: clear goals, efficient execution. The experience of nothingness leads us to doubt stated goals and to be unimpressed by supposed efficiency. Institutions do not exist to be effective, but chiefly to provide reassurance. The role of government (in the American system) is to appear to have goals, to claim to have plans, to create the illusion of effectiveness.

Politics is the realm of illusion. Politics is the restless man's mysticism. It has its own magic, rituals, symbols, doctrines. Politics is the art of power, yes, but it is primarily the art of shaping consciousness. The primary locus of politics is human consciousness. Politics issues from the end of a symbol. Who controls minds controls guns.

1. The Sense of Reality

Institutions (churches, governments, universities, industries, languages) do not exist merely to satisfy pragmatic needs and desires.

Much more fundamentally, they function to construct and to secure a sense of reality. Individuals do not exist first and then, out of certain personal needs, generate institutions.[1] Rather, the functions and roles assumed by individuals in group life generate a sense of reality unique to that group. This special sense of reality structures the needs and desires felt by individuals in the group. Thus, all the key theological words—freedom, justice, community, hope, despair, faith, person—have a different concrete meaning in different societies, and often in different circles in the same society. The housewife in Lake Forest and the housewife in South Chicago have different social images, different social emotions, when they use words like "freedom," "fairness," "despair."

The sense of reality communicated by a lifetime of experiences in one social context may be more or less misleading, more or less open, more or less distorted; it may prepare one well or ill to meet the experience of other human beings from other social contexts. One's sense of reality might be so narrow and fanatical that it positively prevents one from understanding, let alone from having empathy for, the senses of reality of the vast majority of other human beings on this planet.

Human beings make their decisions about what they will willingly die for on the basis of what they take to be real. In quest of a reality that appears to other men as pure illusion, men starve themselves, go joyfully to their deaths, kill themselves. It follows that the sense of reality inculcated in one's own culture may be more or less suicidal. We must, then, be suspicious of the "realism" that governs our universities, industries, and political organs.

Several words are clear tip-offs to our myth. To what do we attach the words "real," "relevant," "reasonable"? Students today are fond of claiming that this or that is "irrelevant," or that this or that is "real." The word "real" is usually used of intense experiences, not of images, concepts, themes, judgments, or even decisions. In particular, students rate intense experiences of community feeling and risk—as in a building seizure or a sit-in—as "the most real" thing they have ever experienced. I conclude that the youth culture is starved for original, spontaneous, unorganized, community experience—seeks it as perhaps our grandfathers on the frontier sought out experience-oriented religious sects. Such large and popular sects, despising dogma and formal ritual and church officialdom, offered vivid experiences of conversion, resolve, and the condemnation of corruption.

The generation of our parents has been perhaps the most organized, pragmatic, least fanatical, most "reasonable" in American history. Rebelling against the raw experience and simple moralism of their parents, our parents accepted pragmatism as a way of life. Compare the smooth, calm operations of Billy Graham with those of Billy Sunday. Note, by contrast, the link between youth culture (dress, manners, dreams) and the folk music and revival tents our grandfathers knew. Note the mountain communes, the love for the simple life, the yen for independence that are common both to youth culture today and to the Americans observed by de Tocqueville in *Democracy in America.*

For the generations of the Depression and the Second World War, the great lesson in life was to avoid the simple moralism of Prohibition, isolationism, America First; to value the high, mature morality of compromise and of small but effective concrete steps. They learned to be suspicious of metaphysical schemes, political utopias, and ideologies composed of shining abstractions that turned out to be murderous in the concrete; to distrust the motives and the intelligence of those who applied the word "moral" to complex social and political affairs. John Foster Dulles spoke often of moral ideals and crusades and sacred callings, as did Whittaker Chambers.

A generation that suffered from such ideals tried to train itself to eliminate moral and religious categories from its practical thinking. The word "real" came to be applied not to intense experiences, or to ardent aspirations, or to spontaneous, community demonstrations of feeling, but to a carefully calculated series of next steps.

"Real" meant "calculated and compromised and effective in the system." Maturity consisted of shifting one's center of gravity from spontaneous moral and religious feelings and from personal experiences to an accurate diagnosis of what was possible in the system, of consequences and compromises that would guarantee effectiveness.

For that generation, the word "relevant" meant "is effective within the system." For the present generation, the word "relevant" means "show me how to live, now, outside the system."

For the former generation, the word "reasonable" meant that a man was objective, calm, cognizant of the consequences of his actions, intent on being effective rather than on "merely" expressing his feelings. For the present generation, "reasonable" is not entirely a coveted description of oneself. The young do not wish to be thought irrational or unreasonable, but they think it reasonable to give priority to feelings, experiences, spontaneities, inner connectedness, and the expression in action of inmost convictions (with or without successful issue).

The sense of reality implied by the way our parents' generation used the words "meaningful," "relevant," "real," and "reasonable" was not so free of myth (or even of passion) as that generation thought.[2] There is no Archimedean point, neutrally poised, from which a man can live without myth, write "at degree zero," take a purely objective view. The myth that dominated the best minds of our parents' generation—often even the minds that thought themselves out of tune with their contemporaries—was the myth of social progress. The world system and the American system were getting better. Considerations of concrete effectiveness and penetrating, objective analysis of functions and operations would lead to further progress. What helped the progress of the system was real, meaningful, relevant, and reasonable.

The unity, aim, and order summed up in the phrase "social progress," by which the preceding generation structured its experience, have been pulled out by the present generation. In the resulting formlessness, many share the experience of nothingness. Unity, aim, and order are now put into experience by "being cool." One must be alert to the ironies and conflicts by which institutions torment, assuage, assist, and trick.[3] The old sense of reality is gone. The institutions of our parents' generation no longer have our spontaneous trust. New institutions have not yet replaced the old. One can give unquestioning allegiance nowhere: one must "keep cool." Have no intense outward feelings; keep one's own counsel; trust no one. Given such distance, speech must chiefly be ironic.

Institutions of government, of social stratification, of economic activity, of science, religion, art, and of family are the chief carriers of a culture's sense of reality. They are its chief means of disciplining young people to the shape of that reality.

One culture's reality is another culture's myth. To know oneself is to be critically aware of the institutions under which one lives. Those institutions shape each individual by the roles into which they channel him, by the tasks, exercises, rewards, and punishments they set before him. Who I am is largely a product of the institutions that have been shaping my perception since the first moments of my existence.

A child today is born like every child since the Stone Age. But then each of us begins immediately to encounter the hospital hygiene and parental styles of mothering appropriate to our social class, economic rank, affective context, and cultural way of life. By the time we are two years old, simply by noting our cries, actions, and expectations, skilled anthropologists can identify quite precisely from which culture and which part of that culture we derive.[4] Before we have a chance to choose for ourselves, anxieties and fears and joys and expectations are a part of our outlook on the world.[5] We notice, or fail to notice, that we are so instructed. Consequently, moment by moment, our culture through its many institutions is trying to teach us its way of imagining reality and conferring maturity, and to turn us away from impulses, feelings, and expectations it has no use for or fears. Who knows how much of the human experience—our own experience—we are obliged to neglect, forget, displace, repress, because it is out of joint with what our culture calls "real" and "mature"?[6] How much of ourselves have we had to disown in order to be where we are today?

The main impact of institutions upon us, in brief, is to organize the chaos of personal experience into a sense of reality. The chief function of social institutions of all sorts and upon all levels is myth-making. Institutions are shapers of experience, perception, value, and action. What they decide is real is enforced as real. What they count important is important. To "drop out" of such institutions is to be "ineffective," that is, "unreal," and either neurotic ("selfish, self-indulgent") or psychotic ("deviant"). Moreover, the enforcers of reality are not merely the policemen and the armies; they are also the loving parents, the smiling teachers, the wonderful psychiatrists, and all those saboteurs of our humanity who try to help us to master the signals and the cues required for our "successful adjustment." Life has already been prearranged; what is real has already been clearly labeled; to be attracted to the unsaid, the unlabeled, the unarranged is to be wild, fanciful, extreme, "interesting," odd, insane, dangerous, subversive. When a young person is being initiated into society, existing norms determine what is to be considered real and what is to be annihilated by silence and disregard. The good, docile student accepts the norms; the recalcitrant student may lack the intelligence—or have too much; may lack maturity—or insist upon being his own man.

If I were to ask a class, "What is that, behind me?" many students would have been well taught to reply, "Obviously, a chair." Nearly all of us live in a world in which as many things as possible already are familiar and have their place, a world prearranged as thoroughly as possible. Few of us often see the chair as a wet winged leather flesh with bended legs swim in chaotic space, coincidence in a billion-year sequence of colliding particles, while we, audience like grasshoppers, sit docilely an entire evening and words drone emptily into our ears. Things are not what they seem. A scientific analysis, a cultural analysis, a carpenter's analysis, a poet's analysis, a madman's analysis tell us discordant stories about that empty, isolated object called a chair. But we do not see its reality—only a sliver of it, an abstraction: "chair." Our perceptual equipment is impoverished; our imagination has been dying day by day since we were six or seven.[7] We are anemic specimens of our race's possibilities.

Our most grievous danger, in fact, is that we live by the most barren and dessicating of myths without even recognizing that it is myth. We have been shaped to be happy with our lot, even proud of it and grateful for it: the nation of progress, God's country. We disparage those primitive peoples who live by myth; we live by science, hardheaded scrutiny, pragmatic sensitivities, facts, and costanalysis. Moreover, in our technical progress we have real, solid, tangible evidence that our way of life is superior. Besides, we have progressed in heroism and happiness. Our marriages are models of mutual communication and unlimited growth in love. Our children understand us, and we them. The routine and paperwork connected with our significant, meaningful jobs are fun. For entertainment, we go to movies, turn on TV, or get into our shining cars; we see the world. We belong to the most interesting social circles. "Wait till you see our new Evinrude." The thought of suicide has never entered our minds.

The truth is that a great many persons in our society have mixed feelings about what used to be called the state of their souls. Life in a capitalist, democratic, pragmatic society is a series of compromises; compromise is a way of life. In our society, commitment, integrity, and purity of heart are weaknesses; they make a person rigid and self-centered; they are hard on the team, the cause, and efficient progress.[8] "The old values" hold sway in fewer and fewer places in American life.[9] But each generation in our recent past has borne along a different sense of reality. The easygoing, rural institutions of our grandparents' time gave way to the scientific bureaucracies of our parents' generation. The myth of common sense, informality, and independent cussedness gave way to the myth of objectivity and technique.

The word "moral" once evoked images of the country, and the word "city" evoked images of corruption. But then Tulsa, Dallas, and Oklahoma City, among others were built around a new science, technology, and affluent bureaucracy.[10] Words like profane, secular, pragmatic, and urban became words signifying progress, maturity, and moral awareness. People who used rural images were living "in the past."

The makers of the powerful present seem to constitute a progressive force; they actually constitute a new establishment desirous of protecting its own sense of reality. They have found it easy to drape their new sense of reality in the conservative symbols of the old sense of reality. "Pioneers" in new industries, they established "new frontiers" through technological advances, "strengthened the free world," and "kept America strong." Thus, the old myths about American life still seem to be usable. Texas industrialists can describe themselves in the favorite patriotic words of Iowa farmers, without noticing that major factors in their own way of life are far outside that of the small farmer: easy money, heavy borrowing, corporate wheeling and dealing, war research, and direct ties to foreign policy.

In academic life and in journalism, the sense of reality practiced by the Texas industrialist receives its intellectual justification. The journalist has been taught to ask questions like "So, what's your next step?" rather than "What other presupposition could you be acting on?" He avoids "theoretical" discussion in favor of "practical" questions—measurable, visible, reportable—and calls the latter "realistic." In academic life, "theological" questions, "metaphysical" questions, "value" questions are less discussed than the "hard," "empirical," "decidable" questions.

The sense of reality favored by American businessmen, military men, journalists, and academicians is remarkably homogeneous. This sense of reality arises from social institutions and has political effects. Those Americans who have come to see that sense of reality as unreal and mythical at first seem to lose their hold on reason, relevance, meaning, and reality. For these words have been preëmpted by the American system. And new institutions, generating a new sense of reality, do not yet exist or are not yet sufficiently powerful. At present, however, it will suffice to show how the institutions of our parents' generation, while boasting of nothing more than their realism, have come to seem unreal.

2. *The Tool*

Rollo May, the distinguished psychoanalyst, described the situation at the end of the 1950s:

With most patients several decades ago (and with naive patients now), we could assume, when they said they had nothing to believe in anymore, that they were suffering from some unconscious conflict about symbols having to do, say, with "God and the authority of father," or "mother and protectiveness" and so on. Our problem then was easier: we had only to help them work through the conflict about their symbols in order that they might choose their own; the dynamic was there. My point is that now, however, patients on a much broader scale seem to be reflecting the general disintegration of cultural symbols, a disintegration that percolates down more and more broadly into the members of society.[11]

He adds: "A decade or so ago the symbols related to 'competitive success' and 'love' did have power to grasp people and elicit their allegiance; but there is reason for believing that these symbols too have lost their power."[12] Love is "more and more identified with security." Yet a man or woman who seeks security is not offering love but dependency. Seeking love for the wrong reasons, people make love impossible to find. Again, the old myth of the rugged, competitive individual has been absorbed by the myth of the organization man, the technician, the member of the team. Love is gone; so also is individuality. The bitterest part, May writes, is that "our patients" have nothing "they can believe in wholeheartedly enough to make commitment of themselves possible."[13] May is not blind to the "emptiness" experienced by so many sensitive persons today: "we often observe in our patients that they cannot discover any accepted symbol in their culture these days sufficiently accepted even to fight against."[14]

Yet May does not conclude that contemporary men lack symbols. He asks:

What do modern people, using our patients for our data still, do when they experience this vacuum of symbols and values? By and large, they try to fill the vacuum with *tools* rather than *symbols*. They seize on signs and techniques borrowed from the scientific and mechanical sphere. It is not surprising, for example, that a plethora of books on sexual *techniques* and *methods* comes out at just the time when people have difficulty experiencing the power of their own emotions and passions with the sexual partner.[15]

The tool becomes the chief symbol for human life. "But the trouble from the psychological side is that when tools and techniques are substituted for genuine symbols, subjectivity is lost. The person may establish some power *over* nature (say, power over his own body, which our patients often desperately seek); but he does so at the price of separating himself ever more fully from nature, including his own body."[16]

The trouble with the leading and most powerful symbol in American culture is that it leads a man to think of himself as an object on which tools are to be used, or as a tool to be used on other objects. Such a symbol makes human value depend on a man's usefulness; the ascription of intrinsic worth becomes impossible. It also excludes too much reality—excludes experiences of honesty, courage, freedom, and community that are not adequately expressed in the language of tools and functions. It is for this reason that the political struggle in America today does not concern power and interests merely, but new perceptions of what is real.

A life without myth is not possible. It is customary today, however, to characterize our own age as one of logic, clarity, and rationality in order to distinguish it from the more primitive, less civilized, more myth-centered cultures of the past. The definitions of myth given in basic dictionaries, for example, record the current viewpoint. *Webster's New Collegiate Dictionary* says:

1. A story, the origin of which is forgotten, ostensibly historical but usually such as to explain some practice, belief, institution, or natural phenomenon. Myths are especially associated with religious rites and beliefs. 2. A person or thing existing only in imagination. 3. Such legends collectively; legendary or mythical matter.

The Random House Dictionary emphasizes even more strongly the independence of myth from any basis in fact or natural explanation; it emphasizes the uncritical, fictitious, unproven, and inauthentic character of myth:

1. a traditional or legendary story, usually concerning some superhuman being or some alleged person or event, with or without a determinable basis of fact or a natural explanation, esp., a traditional or legendary story that is concerned with deities or demigods and the creation of the world and its inhabitants. 2. stories or matters of this kind: *in the realm of myth.* 3. any invented story, idea, or concept: *His rationalizations of his failings are pure myth.* 4. an imaginary or fictitious thing or person. 5. an unproved collective belief that is accepted uncritically and is used to justify a social institution, as the belief in the biological inferiority of slaves used in support of slave societies.

These records of our common usage suggest, however, that a culture that defines myth in this way is attempting to show its own superiority over cultures governed by legends or stories it no longer credits, and is blind to the myths that dominate its own consciousness. Those myths, moreover, are clearly revealed in the recorded definitions.

Modern myths are the stories of enlightenment, of the emergence of the individual from the collective, of the preeminence of fact, natural explanation, critical reason, and proof. Yet the modern myth recorded unconsciously by these dictionaries does not adequately express our modern experience: the dropping of the atomic bombs on Japan; a daily "body count" in Vietnam (which never adds up to the weekly totals, and yet over time states that we have killed three times more of the enemy than we say exists); the vast wealth of this nation and the uses made of it. Are we an enlightened culture? Are the facts about us facts or only our preferred myths? Have the intensive development of critical reason, empirical methods, and technical skills in our college professors, for example, provided a distinctly superior and attractive type of human being? Modern America has its own myths, but it perfers to think of them as rational and realistic. And that precisely is the function of myth: *not* to appear as "merely a myth," but to shape one's selection of what is rational and what is real.

Claude Levi-Strauss has shown that so-called primitive peoples are no less logical than modern people in understanding and acting according to their own myths.[17] It is a mistake to think of our mental habits as logical and theirs as mythical. Our myth happens to be a myth aimed at acquiring power over nature and of controlling our environment efficiently. It is a moot point whether our myth is morally superior to myths aimed primarily at reconciling men both to the irrationalities of existence and to one another.

A particularly striking paragraph on the logical structure of current scientific myths occurs in an essay of Werner Heisenberg, the nuclear physicist:

The aim of research is thus no longer knowledge of the atoms and their motion "in themselves," separated from our experimental questioning; rather, right from the beginning, we stand in the center of the confrontation between nature and man, of which science, of course, is only a part. The familiar classification of the world into subject and object, inner and outer world, body and soul, somehow no longer quite applies, and indeed leads to difficulties. In science, also, the object of research is no longer nature in itself but rather nature exposed to man's questioning, and to this extent man here also meets himself.[18]

The modern American myth unites two streams in the history of science: "The claim of science to be capable of reaching out into the whole cosmos . . . is mirrored in technology which step by step penetrates new realms, transforms our environment before our eyes, and impresses our image upon it."[19] Science aims at understanding nature as a whole; technology aims at enlarging man's power. These aims, Heisenberg notes, are "little questioned." They "coalesce in the banal slogan: 'Knowledge is power.' "[20]

No secret is deeper in the American soul, it appears, than the desire for mastery through knowledge. In the wake of the successful flight of Apollo 8 around the moon, the most penetrating recent fulfillment of the myth until the actual landing on the moon, the hearts of scientists, editorialists, and men in the street were stirred. *Time* echoed the prologues and epilogues of a thousand textbooks in science and technology these last fifty years:

For this is what Westernized man can do. He will not turn into a passive, contemplative being; he will not drop out and turn off; he will not seek stability and inner peace in the quest for nirvana. Western man is Faust, and if he knows anything at all, he knows how to challenge nature, how to dare against dangerous odds and even against reason. He knows how to reach for the moon. . . . That is Western man, and with these qualities he will succeed or fail.[21]

But the myth of the tool and the technique is getting harder and harder to believe. Thus *Time* had to turn to apologetics:

It is possible to look at the moon flight and shudder at the vast, impersonal, computerized army of interchangeable technicians who brought it about. It is also possible to see in this endeavor the crucial gifts or organization and cooperation that alone will make survival in the post-industrial age feasible. It is possible to look at the moon flight and be dismayed at the crass expenditure of money, sweat and time, the sheer materialist effort, the ultimate triumph of gadgetry, the unabashed hubris of technique. But it is also possible to see in it the genius that is providing the abundance to end poverty, and the order and precision that may yet bring peace—or at least bring it somewhat nearer.[22]

There is no doubt about the power of the American myth. It conquers every myth it meets. Its power is not merely over the mind, however. It produces power for the hands: centralized governments, industries, armies, cities, sciences, research facilities. It may be that the American myth appeals to the desire for empire—to ambition, to profit, and to greed—more fundamentally than it appeals to the mind or to humanitarian purposes. The history of industrialization and modernization is not, in any case, an altogether happy commentary on the humanity of a culture that has embraced the myth of knowledge as power. Moreover, the myth is not limited to Americans. Although we exemplify it most totally, it is a European, Western myth. Thus Harold Lasswell writes:

The civilization of Western Europe is distinguished by certain attitudes which survive the most varied local developments, and impose themselves upon successive generations. European civilization is activistic: it fosters the manipulation of man and nature; it favors the externalizing rather than the internalizing of human impulses. European civilization is parochial: it fosters local loyalties, like nationalism, and curbs the tendency to assert functional loyalties as a means of universal union. European civilization has the expectation of violence; it takes wars, revolutions, secessions, revolts, gang struggles, and homicide for granted; regardless of how violence may be deplored, the probability of violence is sorrowfully assumed by the overwhelming majority. There are other cultures ("primitive" cultures) which take none of these things for granted. But the Western European pattern now holds most of mankind in its clutches.[23]

Those young Americans who have served abroad in the Peace Corps or with International Voluntary Services and other such organizations have learned through their own experience that middle class Americans are not more intelligent, more logical, more subtle, more rich and varied in their emotional life, more developed in their sense of humor, more compassionate, more intuitive, more perceptive, more at home in their own bodies, more "connected" to their environment than "underdeveloped" peoples. The rebel guerrillas fighting in Vietnam against unspeakable technological odds have not shown themselves less intelligent, less courageous, less brilliant than American soldiers who are college graduates. Black men in this country have long held in their hearts and minds truths about the blindness, corruption, and repression of the American way of life that few white persons can bear to face.[24]

The universities, we saw earlier, are the primary myth-making institution in our society. They have, by and large, been leaders in promoting the perspective of tools and techniques as the myth through which to structure our experience, our learning, and our actions. What Rollo May describes as true of the 1920s is no longer accurate, although it does mirror a tendency that has not yet been overcome, a tendency

to rule symbols out as much as possible (except a few sign-symbols in science and mathematics), never to raise the topics of symbols or myths if it could be helped, and otherwise to regard symbols as temporary concessions to our ignorance in matters which we should soon be able to describe in clear, rational terms. We left these esoteric topics to the poets and literary critics. Neither term, symbol or myth, even appears in the index of the standard psychology textbook—written not by a Watsonian behaviorist but by a dynamic psychologist who was certainly enlightened and broad of interest—which my class and many similar classes studied in colleges throughout the country. We tried to be "hardheaded" men, as Alfred North Whitehead put it in his essay cited in this volume, who "want facts and not symbols," and who therefore "push aside symbols as being mere makebelieves, veiling and distorting that inner sanctuary of truth which reason claims as its own."[25]

The tendency toward hardheadedness persists. Surely it is fair to notice that "hardheadedness" is itself a symbol, and that the story of the man who resolutely "pushes aside symbols" and enters the "inner sanctuary of truth" is itself a myth. In the name of knowledge, power, and effectiveness, millions must shape themselves into creatures of "analytic reason."[26] Yet analytic reason carries with it such wealth, such prestige, such power, and it is so deeply reinforced by the needs of our society, that as a myth it seems virtually impregnable.

The key to American politics is the American sense of reality. The schools are the primary guardians of that sense of reality. (The schools, revolutionaries need to note, are not, however, the most powerful guardians; in at least two ways, economic institutions are far more powerful than educational institutions. First, the rewards and penalties the former mete out tutor even the young to what "really" counts in society, no matter what the schools might say. Secondly, those with economic power ultimately have a stranglehold on the economic resources supposedly needed for education today. They give monies and they take away, according to their own priorities).

As one might expect, American schools seduce young people into the sense of reality best suited to American social and political priorities. Jerome S. Bruner of Harvard, probably the nation's foremost educational theoretician, has made famous the notion that education should proceed from the outside in. What metaphor does he choose to structure human experience? The tool. Bruner's idea is that tools and techniques shape the brain. To learn society's tool systems is to unlock one's own mind so that it can grow. Bruner cites "The Washburn hypothesis" from a paper presented at the one-hundredth anniversary of Darwin's *Origin of Species:*

It would now appear . . . that the large size of the brain of certain hominids was a relatively late development and that the brain evolved due to new selection pressures *after* bipedalism and consequent upon the use of tools. The tool using, ground living, hunting way of life created the large human brain rather than a large brained man discovering certain new ways of life. We believe this conclusion is the most important result of the recent fossil hominid discoveries and is one which carries far-reaching implications for the interpretation of human behavior and its origin. . . .

The uniqueness of modern man is seen as the result of a technical-social life which tripled the size of the brain, reduced the face, and modified many other structures of the body.[27]

Bruner concludes that "the principle change in man over a long period of years—perhaps five hundred thousand years—has been alloplastic rather than autoplastic." That is, man has changed by linking himself with new external tool systems rather than by conspicuous change from within. "What is significant about the growth of mind in the child is to what degree it depends not upon capacity but upon the unlocking of capacity by techniques that came from exposure to the specialized environment of a culture."[28] Richard M. Jones, in *Fantasy and Feeling in Education*, accuses Bruner of favoring skills that lead students to adjust too easily to their environment, rather than skills which are disturbing, unsettling, noninstrumental, and creative.[29]

In any case, American schools are not characteristically interested in the depth of their students' fantasy life, the complexity of their emotions, the delicacy of their sensitivity, the variety and range of their instincts—only in their capacity to store information and to analyze information. In an outrageous essay, "The Student as Nigger," Jerry Farber describes the plight of young men and young women who, during their emotionally and sexually most vital years, are constantly addressed as if they were computers.[30] It does not concern the school whether the students' minds are imaginative, questioning, dreamy, lusty, impulsive, or unconventional. The school cares only whether their activities mirror the analytic skills required for our science, technology, and industry. Who they are—their subjectivity—is left out. Our society detains its adolescents in a rigid institutional structure longer than any other known society.[31] Thus the students have little recourse but to submit to the indignities and learn to like them.

The students, despite widespread hopes, prove too inexperienced to know exactly what is wrong with the schools, let along which remedies are authentic. They often make the natural, adolescent mistake of rebelling against intelligence itself in the name of feeling, experience, instinct, impulse, sensitivity, community, action, or all of these together. Those among them who are affluent do not have to become good at anything; with a little help from their friends, they can get along for as many years as they care to foresee. They need think of nothing more than today. They have been told so often how unique they are that some feel free to manifest an unsurpassed moral and intellectual arrogance; their ignorance protects them from second thought. These few may have rescued the tradition of the Know-Nothings from oblivion.

We stand in need of a new sense of reality, a new image of how to be intelligent, sensitive, and free. We cannot count on students achieving that sense for us; we must create it ourselves. What James, Peirce, and Dewey had accomplished by 1910 needs to be accomplished again: the articulation of a style of American life that might liberate our national energies for the next fifty years—in the same way the myth of pragmatism has for the last fifty.

There were grave inadequacies in the pragmatic sense of reality, as we discover to our cost today. Pragmatism systematically misled us, both in our attempts to understand ourselves and in our way of perceiving other cultures. We took the tool as our favorite image of ourselves, and applied ourselves to mastering the earth, accepting some obscure call of destiny. We looked at others as candidates, less highly developed than we, for becoming like ourselves. We did not notice our inner emptiness, our pleasure in violence, our capacity to bore others and ourselves. We wanted other men to love us for working to turn the whole world into New Jersey.

The problem is how to conceive a vision that might displace pragmatism from the center of the national psyche.

3. Politics and Consciousness

The strength of the analytic mind when it turns to the study of power in institutions, that is to say to politics, is its emphasis upon the "hard facts" of interest and power.[32] Its weakness is its lack of concern for the symbols that determine what constitutes (a) a fact, (b) a significant trend, and (c) the culminating value toward which or from which events are perceived as moving. Lasswell writes as follows in his short, pungent summary, *Politics: Who gets What, When, How?:* "An institution is a pattern of 'practices'; and a practice is a pattern of 'perspectives' (symbols) and 'operations.'

Taken in the aggregate all perspectives of an institution constitute its 'myth'; all operations are its 'technique.' "[33]

In general, liberal and pragmatic political writers in America tend to concentrate upon operations and technique and to ignore myth and symbol. Yet the most fundamental source of political power and influence is the structuring of reality inculcated in babies from birth. "Constituted authority perpetuates itself by shaping the consciences of those who are born within its sphere of control," Lasswell writes. "Hence the great revolutions are in defiance of emotions which have been directed by nurses, teachers, guardians, and parents along 'accredited' channels of conscience."[34] In order to take part in a revolution, therefore, a man must first do battle with his own instincts; he must rupture his own conscience. "When the political order works smoothly, the masses venerate the symbols; the elite . . . suffers from no withering sense of immorality."[35] When people have to think about renewing basic convictions, or finding new symbols, the society's sense of reality has already decayed; in periods of "health," that sense is purely and simply obvious to everybody.

So deep are flourishing cultural myths, in fact, that no conspiracy is needed to maintain them; virtually everyone "accepts reality as it is," and the elites are full of confidence. The culture's way of life molds every aspect of human life into its own form of reality. "The individualism of bourgeois society like the communism of a socialized state must be inculcated from the nursery to the grave."[36] Children are given penny banks; at school, they trade baseball cards; in the classroom each individual is given a mark to set him over against his fellows. "Success and failure depend on you." Almost every human encounter reinforces myths like the primacy of economics, competition, work, and thrift. Lasswell collects further examples:

. . . money is scarce and "it is not wise to buy the bicycle now"; "we must be economical and keep the old car another season"; "they're headed for the poorhouse; have you seen how she dresses!"; "they had a falling out over the will"; "she really married him for his money"; "some say he poisoned her so he could collect the insurance"; "he was a brilliant man but he took to drink and went to the dogs"; "he was a good provider until he went running around spending his money on loose women"; "I hear Harry is making a good thing of it in real estate"; "How much did that cost you?"; "how much is the tuition at that college?"[37]

Portraits of the successful—usually business executives—hang on walls, and their presence dignifies banquets and gatherings; appropriate comments point out that those who beg, steal, or don't work are "failures." Everything—gossip, fiction, teaching, conversation, movies—drive home the theme of personal responsibility. "He failed because he lacked tact or had halitosis or didn't go to the right college or forgot to slick down his hair. She was successful because she got the right shade of lipstick, took French lessons at home on the phonograph, kept the skin you love to touch, and bought soft and subtle kinds of lingerie. If she took up typewriting and shorthand, she would marry the boss."[38]

Moreover, Lasswell continues, "Social and industrial difficulties are automatically traced to personal equations."[39] The owner or manager is held responsible for everything that happens. Trouble is always due to "agitators" or racketeers. "The form of attention is thus absorbed by personal problems. . . . The newspapers report that he won an election because he made a smart speech. The newspapers report that he got killed because he forgot to look to see if the train was coming. The newspapers report that she got hurt because she did not read the instructions on the package."[40] The newspapers do not write about social conditions, whole contexts, complex relationships. The American ideology, oblivious to fact, stresses the centrality of the individual. Not unemployment, crop failure, or inefficiency due to government regulations, "but motives and struggles are the subject matter of the secondary means of communication in the bourgeois world. When such an ideology impregnates life from start to finish, the thesis of collective responsibility runs against a wall of noncomprehension."[41]

We are so thoroughly conditioned to our own myths of personal struggle and personal responsibility that we can hardly imagine, let alone understand, the reality of community life and community responsibility among such other peoples as Africans, Chinese, and Russians. We imagine other people to be living under a bombardment of propaganda and conditioning, but we scarcely notice how thorough our own conditioning is, and how deeply into our psyches it has sunk. We have been taught that our institutions are superior to those of others; so have the people of every other nation.

The experience of nothingness teaches a man the poverty and the limitations of all symbols. It teaches him to look with skepticism upon perceptions and values that others take for granted. Thus those who have shared the experience of nothingness are the most profoundly subversive of all dissenters; for they deny, not this or that institutional arrangement, but the prevailing sense of reality. Their conscience is out of tune with the conscience of the dominant elites, as well as out of tune with the corresponding conscience of those ordinary people who still have faith in the elites.[42] "[Every] elite defends and asserts itself in the name of symbols of the common destiny."[43] All elites act in the name of peace, prosperity, national prestige, progress, justice, liberty, the common good, and so on.[44] Moreover, they ordinarily try to respect the sense of reality of the ordinary people, so as not to alarm them or frighten them.

In the United States, there is a tradition of respect for influential elites: for presidents and cabinet officers, public officials and heads of corporations, chancellors and professors. Deference is paid such persons. Their words are accepted as truthful. Their stated purposes are taken to be identical with their latent purposes. To be sure, no political order can be established or maintained without a bond of basic trust. To be sure, Americans indulge in personal criticism of public officials, and lampoon them in cartoons and in countless jokes and anecdotes; we have a strong tradition of irreverence. Still, newspapers, commentators, and most public voices emphasize personal characteristics, personal struggles, and personal weaknesses;

they assume that the institutions, the processes of reform, and the context in which American elites operate are fundamentally humane. Such personalization of institutional life probably makes Americans believe that they have far more control over their own social systems than they do.[45] The inadequacy of personal efforts is only slowly beginning to dawn upon us. The helplessness so widely felt in 1968 was not merely the temporary lesson of an unusually painful year. It was a more truthful perception of the inadequacy of the present form of our democratic institutions. They do not give us the control over our destiny that they symbolize. Much more than our popular stories allow, events and institutions master us.

Murray Edelman has tried to analyze how myths and symbols structure our perception of political realities.[46] In *The Symbolic Uses of Power,* he shows many of the methods employed by public officials in the United States to give us a sense of participation, of action accomplished, and of steps taken, even on occasions when careful analysis reveals that no progress has been made at all, or even that the situation has worsened. His point is not so much that the mass media deceives us; it is rather that even our political analysts, our teachers, the agents involved, and we ourselves work the deception. We want to believe certain things about ourselves and our way of life. Particularly, we want to boast that we are free, and that we control our own destiny.

With help from Edelman and others, I list a series of myths we wish to believe about ourselves, which are patently not true. The first:

We wish to believe that, because we vote every two years, our elected government legitimately represents us. In fact, our voting has little power to affect the main power factors in American life. School teachers, good government groups like the League of Women Voters, and candidates themselves never tire of repeating that voting gives the people control over their officials and policies, that the citizen who fails to vote should not complain if he gets poor government, and that elections are fundamental to democracy. But, rather paradoxically, the voting behavior studies have shown that issues are a minor determinant to how people cast their ballots, most voters being quite ignorant of what the issues are and of which party stands for what position. We also know from studies of legislative and administrative behavior that neither of these depends primarily upon election outcomes. So what people get does not depend mainly on their votes.

. . . successful political professionals have evidently long acted on the assumption that there is in fact relatively little familiarity [with issues], that expressions of deep concern are rare, that quiescence is common, and that, in general, the congressman can count upon stereotyped reactions rather than persistent, organized pursuit of material interests on the part of most constituents.

Lazarsfeld and his associates concluded from their voting behavior studies that propagandistic language used in the course of election campaigns serves chiefly to arouse voting predispositions rather than to change voting intentions or behavior.[47]

The American electoral system is not in practice—realistically speaking, perhaps, cannot be—what theory would have it be. Even the vaunted stability of the American electoral system may be due to a lack of imagination and justice; it is an unflattering continuation of a centrist coalition of the status quo. Before and after an election, virtually the same type of man fills a given office. Before and after an election, virtually the same powerful groups remain everywhere in virtually identical positions. In a swiftly changing world, the structural rigidity of our democracy may lead to disaster.

Secondly, Americans wish to believe that government is a neutral, detached, scrutinizing agency in controversial affairs. In fact, those who staff governmental regulatory agencies are almost always persons from the industry being regulated. Men go from industry into government, and out again; the personnel of the two worlds are virtually indistinguishable. The government is not an independent group of men, but rather like a shelter in which the same men come and go. Not surprisingly, studies by Edelman and others show that the consequence of establishing a regulatory agency is in most cases to legitimize, to clarify, and to facilitate the very activities that the agency was founded to check.[48]

Thirdly, Americans wish to believe that their leaders control events. The fact is that the chief role of leadership is that of symbolic reassurance.[49] Leaders need not do anything. But they need to give the appearance of being hard at work, on top of events, and in control. Midnight meetings are held, urgent news conferences are called, dramatic trips are made—in order to make leadership visible rather than to make it effective. Most of the serious problems of our society are beyond the powers of our leaders, but the myth of leaders cutting huge swathes in national problems seems important to our sense of meaning. (Senator Eugene McCarthy understood this point in his campaign in 1968, but was called "lazy" or "a nihilist" when he acted upon it.)

Fourthly, Americans wish to believe that administrators are responsive to their concerted pressure, if not to their needs. But the fact is that the relations between administrators and citizens are governed by tacit rules, outlining a well-accepted game.[50] Great public pressure results in a great public gesture, as ineffectual as possible, and the public is almost always satisfied. There is even an inverse relation between administrative gesture and administrative action. The more effective the action, the less is said about it; the more dramatic the pledge, the less effective the intended actions.[51] Thus legislation challenging powerful elites is often long on publicity, short on effect. A great deal is said about poverty and race; actual changes are few. For years, little was said about military expenditure; the growth rate was powerful. Enormous waste, loss, and theft in the military are taken for granted; a one per cent annual loss in poverty funds is made to appear scandalous.

Another example of the elaborate game between administrators and citizens is law enforcement. The strict enforcement of laws is intolerable; so is flagrant disrespect for law. The speeding motorist is not caught every time, or even penalized every time; but when reprimanded he should nod his head and look serious. For it is the symbolic power of law that police monitor, not actual behavior.[52] The Black Panthers violate the symbols openly.

Sixth, Americans wish to believe that events have a logic, that actions have consequences, and that history teaches specific lessons. But in fact political events have a metaphorical meaning to one group that may be totally different from the meaning they have for another. A succession of conspicuous events in the news sets up routine signals for role-making and symbolization, which are perceived quite differently by different groups.[53] What does political event X mean? Your answer is your myth.

Seventh, Americans like to believe that the terms or names of political goals—like "Peace with honor" or "An end to poverty"— are a key to the determination of policy; and that certain ends or values are selected, and then instrumental, pragmatic means followed. But in fact the terms or names of goals are not chosen because they direct, control, or predict behavior, but because of their symbolic power. Existing interest groups clash and bargain, and behavior follows from the adjustment of past arrangements. The public is suspicious of bargaining, however, so both sides cover their actual behavior by hortatory language using the terms or names of symbolic goals.[54] Both sides evince loyalty to the symbols, but the symbols are not intended to guide behavior so much as to tell a story the public wishes to believe. Similarly, activities of secret agents, the presence of military power, and unwitting involvements often guide the accumulative foreign policy and operations of government; goals and purposes serve as later covers rather than as predictive guides.

Eighth, Americans like to believe that political language points to political attitudes, positions, and arguments. In fact, the primary function of political language is to carry out a public ritual, satisfying basic social instincts.[55] Certain key words repeated again and again are mentally restful to political audiences. To attack the prevailing symbol structure of a group is to awaken the threat of chaos. It is also to arouse intense opposition, whose intensity is not measured by the power of the attacker but by the depth of the emotion aroused. Stokely Carmichael had little "real" power, but great symbolic power, and he set many deep tides in motion.

In these ways and many more, institutions are what their perceivers wish them to be. Their life in the psyches of the community is their main source of power, stability, and reality. When sufficient numbers of members of the community begin to think differently, those institutions lose their power, stability, and reality. The trappings of power may remain. But new formations gather just below the public surface; in some cases, chaos itself threatens. Institutions need myths and symbols that hold the trust of people; without trust, men must be on guard against each other in the night. The fundamental tragedy of Vietnam, for example, is the dissolution of trust; no available myth or symbol or person commands general allegiance. Naked power for a while sways peasants this way, and then that, from season to season, day to night. No doubt new symbols —"Peace"—gather beneath the surface.

4. Nothingness and Reality

Paul Tillich has warned: "All the talk about the 'new myth' is an indication of how remote the new myth is in actuality. A myth that is sought for as myth is for the very reason repelled. Only when one's thinking has objective reference can a truly mythical element pulsate through it."[56] Today pluralism—rendering every parochial sense of reality less than compelling—provides the objective reference that makes the experience of nothingness frequent and powerful. Similarly, technological development provides the objective reference that grounds a pervasive new myth, a new sense of reality.

Radical thinkers today are seldom Luddites, seldom antitechnological, seldom pastoral romantics. Quite the contrary.[57] Without affluence and technology the current radical movement is not conceivable; without electric guitars, motorcycles, stereo sets, television, and films the new consciousness would not have arisen. Without social and intellectual mobility at home, travel abroad, fearlessness regarding hunger, shelter, and employment, and a general confidence that the basic material problems of existence have been solved, a new sense of reality would not have a basis in fact. *The new consciousness has technology at its foundation. It places technology in the context of, and at the service of, human consciousness.* It achieves this by displacing analytic reason, the myth of objectivity, the conception of knowledge as power, and pragmatism (narrowly construed) from the inmost to the outer circles of consciousness. The symbol for man is not a tool. The story of man is not adequately expressed by an expert in a white coat, a technician, a machine.

What, then, is the new myth? The new sense of reality has as its ground the experience of nothingness. That is to say, it recognizes the emptiness, terror, and formlessness at the center of human consciousness. It also recognizes that a man glimpses the emptiness, terror, formlessness, only by virtue of his honesty and courage. In the exercise of his freedom, he is indebted to the accumulated insights of his community. Consequently the experience of nothingness is not paralyzing—it is liberating. In its dark light, nothing is beyond questioning, sacred, immobile. On the other hand, since that dark light springs from honesty, courage, freedom, and community, everything in life that promotes these qualities becomes precious and sacred. The sense of reverence that disappears when totems and taboos perish is regained when honesty, courage, freedom, and community are cherished.

The choice to remain faithful to the drive to question (the fertile source of the experience of nothingness) brings with it an obscure joy. For to be faithful to that drive—to allow it to function as the integrator of one's senses, instincts, sensibilities, emotions, perspectives, insights, judgments, and actions—is to be constantly expanding one's horizon, constantly losing one's life, and constantly regaining it. It is to be as alert to other persons, to situations, and to events as one can: to their fragility and terror, as well as to their obscure coherences and often veiled beauty. To be faithful to the drive to question is to accept despair as one's due, to accept risk as one's condition, and to accept the crumbs of discovery as joy.

The darkness is habitable: that is the first message of the new consciousness. It is *in*habited: that is its discovery. Those who seek security could not, to assuage their need, amass to themselves enough objects, or persons treated like objects, even if they had all of history at their disposal. Those who accept the darkness as their lot are instantly secure, not through some newfound solidity but through the perception that insecurity is man's natural state, a truthful state, a healthy state. That is why St. John of the Cross writes, in the poem set as the prologue to these lectures: "In darkness and secure." He means: "Secure *because* in darkness, for everywhere else lie illusions and falsehoods. To rest here is to rest in truth."

St. John writes, "In the *happy* night." And he continues:

> *This light guided me More surely than the light of noonday,*
> *To the place where he (well I knew who!) was awaiting me—*
> *A place where none appeared.*

The case is not prejudiced in favor of the theist or in favor of the atheist. For both there is the same darkness. Both follow the drive to question to the place—the place where the believer runs forward to greet well he knows who; the place where, as the atheist expects, none appears; the place where there is silence brighter than the noonday.

The myth appropriate to the new time requires a constant return to inner solitude, an unbroken awareness of the emptiness at the heart of consciousness. It is a harsh refusal to allow idols to be placed in the sanctuary. It requires also a scorching gaze upon all those bureaucracies, institutions, manipulators, symbol-makers, and hucksters who employ technology and its supposed realities to bewitch and bedazzle the psyche. Countless numbers of men in a technological society are hired to keep goods moving, those goods pouring from the machines, hired to bark and bellow and rage and cajole. They are hired to sell.

To sell they must lie. They must try to trap the resources of the psyche and turn them toward consumer goods: a girl's loins the fenders of a shiny car, a deodorant a forbidden adventure, a toothpaste utter joy, a politician God's humble son. They also use subtle lies: a Ph.D. for accepting the professional sense of reality, a cabinet post in order to make your insights more effective, a job to blunt your discontent.

Who are you? What do you want? Society's sense of reality? The sun also rises. Vanity.

The experience of nothingness grounds the minimal necessary skepticism to survive as a man of integrity today. Without it, the machines, the myth-makers sink their hands into one's soul.

The experience of nothingness arms a man against his own puritanism, his desire to be perfect, and his despair at not being able to be honest, courageous, free, or brotherly. Who is he (who is at his center nothing) to be dismayed because his actions prove his worthlessness? The self is not at the center of the universe. The sun shines no less brilliantly, the skies are no more thickly gray because he has betrayed his resolve. A man is too insignificant to be preoccupied with his own failures. Whatever energy he has is required for attending to the loneliness, the pain, the needs of others. No contrition is more truthful than other-centeredness. To contract one's horizon in sorrow helps neither oneself nor others. To make failures the occasion of more sensitive attention to others is to turn decline into growth.

The experience of nothingness is a powerful weapon against pragmatists, reformers, political machines, dictators, judges, and officials of every sort. For their powers, though real, are not ultimate, as they would have us believe. Over the experience of nothingness itself, and the sources whence it springs, they have no power. Illusions they can take away. What is ultimately real they cannot touch. It is beyond their competence.

The experience of nothingness generates both revolution and reform. It generates reform, where reform is possible, when the myth upon which abuses rest is shattered by honesty. And where the energy or the machinery for reform are lacking, the experience of nothingness is the ground from which revolutionaries draw the strength to fight against great odds, and even to die, in order to protect the streams of honesty, courage, freedom, and brotherliness that nourish it.

When institutions pollute these streams, those who share the experience of nothingness do not stand in awe of the false claims made upon them. They know that all institutions justify themselves and their procedures in the name of symbols and myths of man's common destiny. But all such symbols and myths must withstand the fires of the experience of nothingness. Those that do not burn away deserve respect. The promotion of conditions in which men can with increasing frequency become honest, courageous, free, and brotherly is the criterion by which institutions are judged. Institutions have no other purpose.

The sources of the experience of nothingness are dynamic. They are also communal. Consequently, they have social and political power of the greatest importance. The new consciousness, arising from its base in a technological society, passes judgment upon the myth of the tool and the technician, upon the liberal capitalistic, democratic society (as well as upon its socialist mirror image). In the name of the experience of nothingness the new consciousness propels men to invention, discovery, and growth.

Evolution did not stop yesterday. And it often proceeds by sudden quantum leaps; it is not always reformist merely, but new and revolutionary. At a certain level, tensions sometimes build until the membrane breaks and forms of life spill out into a whole new sphere, along a new axis. We are in need of such a leap. The institutions of the present do not embody adequate myths; they become increasingly unreal. There is a growing sense of reality, a new reality, that awaits new institutions to give it shape. "In darkness and in concealment," those who labor to build the new institutions are at present in maximum insecurity.

Their labors will be long. Mao-tse-Tung lay in wait, toiling daily at routine jobs, for twenty years until the time was ripe. The revolution begun by Ho Chi Minh in 1920 was not yet completed at his death. Few voyagers enter the promised land they seek.

The experience of nothingness arms one against those who shout "crisis," insist on "now," and warn that "we only have ten years, if that." (Who ever promised us the world would not end? Suppose the human race expires at 3 A.M., March 11, 1983. Until then is there a better way to live than faithful to the experience of nothingness, to honesty, courage, freedom and community?) To depend upon emotions of crisis is all too American. The rhythms of evangelists —even if today dressed like professors—too easily touch us. No worthwhile revolution is built on instant passions. Those taught by the experience of nothingness trust nothing but the slow, accumulating work of countless skillful men and women. A revolution is a tide of skillful laborers, not amateurs but perfectionists, working with boldness, courage, steadiness. Steadiness is everything. "Beware the crisis mongers!"

Moreover, guided in the night by the experience of nothingness, many expect that the new myth, the new institutions, will not be beyond questioning. Like the old myths and the old institutions, they, too, will have to bear the heat. They, too, will prove inadequate.

It is through one small step after another that the human pilgrimage, wherever it will end, proceeds. No grand assault upon utopia is possible. No utopia withstands the experience of nothingness. There is no resting place. Yet the toil is not like that of Sisyphus.[58] It is not a rock we push. What we push is not inanimate but capable of growth.

It is our courage. Courage grows by exercise, and horizons, personal and communal, expand. The eyes of Sisyphus were scornful. But the eyes of those kindled by the experience of nothingness reflect exactly the honesty, courage, freedom, and community their possessors choose to live.

Notes

1. The Experience of Nothingness

1. My purpose is not altogether different from that of Josiah Royce, in one of the first volumes of the Bross Library, *The Sources of Religious Insight* (New York: Scribner's, 1912).

2. "Where family and nation once stood, or Church and Party, there will be hospital and theater too, the normative institutions of the next culture. . . . Religious man was born to be saved; psychological man is born to be pleased. The difference was established long ago, when 'I believe,' theory of the ascetic, lost precedence to 'one feels,' the caveat of the therapeutic. And if the therapeutic is to win out, then surely the psychotherapist will be his secular spiritual guide." Philip Rieff, *The Triumph of the Therapeutic: Uses of Faith After Freud* (New York: Harper & Row, Harper Torchbooks, 1966), pp. 24-25.

3. Sidney Hook says the question asked by Schelling and Heidegger, "Why is there something: why is there not nothing?" is "devoid of sense except as a sign of emotional anxiety." *The Quest for Being*, (New York: St. Martin's Press, 1961), p. 147.

4. Charles Frankel, *The Love of Anxiety and Other Essays* (New York: Dell, Delta, 1967), pp. 1-11.

5. "Developed societies may well experience, in the not-too-distant future, occupational and geographical migrations or internal conflicts whose disruptive effects will dwarf those now occurring in non-developed lands. What ecological tragedies may not await the United States, generated by the very 'success' it has had in industrializing and producing goods efficiently? Will these be less destructive than those suffered by the victims of nature's ecological caprices (droughts, floods, plagues)? While it is easy for us to measure the high price paid for remaining underdeveloped, we lack instruments to gauge the price paid for the vaunted 'efficiency' attendant upon development." Denis Goulet, "Development for What?," *Comparative Political Studies*, July 1968, p. 303.

6. See my *Theology for Radical Politics* (New York: Herder & Herder, 1969).

7. Siegfried Kraucauer, *Theory of Film* (New York: Oxford University Press, 1965).

8. Roland Barthes, *Writing Degree Zero*, (London: Jonathan Cape, 1967).

9. Contrast Dietrich Bonhoeffer: "Religious people speak of God when human knowledge (perhaps simply because they are too lazy to think) has come to an end, or when human resources fail—in fact it is always the *deus ex machina* that they bring on to the scene, either for the apparent solution of insoluble problems, or as strength in human failure—always, that is to say, exploiting human weakness or human boundaries. . . . It always seems to me that we are trying anxiously in this way to reserve some space for God; I should like to speak of God not on the boundaries but at the centre, not in weakness but in strength; and therefore not in death and guilt but in man's life and goodness." *Letters and Papers From Prison*, rev. ed. (New York: Macmillan paperback, 1967), p. 142.

10. See Jean-Paul Sartre, "The Desire to be God," in *Existentialism and Human Emotions* (New York: Philosophical Library, 1957), pp. 60–67.

11. Friedrich Nietzsche, *The Will to Power*, ed. Walter Kaufmann (New York: Random House, 1967), p. 9.

12. Albert Camus, *The Myth of Sisyphus and Other Essays* (New York: Random House, Vintage Books, 1960), p. 38.

13. Nietzsche, *op. cit.*, pp. 12–13.

14. Here I depart from Nietzsche's words. His sentence reads: ". . . and a soul that longs to admire and revere has wallowed in the idea of some supreme form of domination and administration (—if the soul be that of logician, complete consistency and real dialectic are quite sufficient to reconcile it to everything)." *Ibid.*

15. Experience, R. D. Laing writes, is neither "subjective" nor "objective," neither "inner" nor "outer." In ordinary and scholarly discourse, "inner" and "outer" distinguish between experience and behavior. "More accurately this is a distinction between different modalities of experience, namely, perception (as outer) in contrast to imagination, etc. (as inner). But perception, imagination, fantasy, reverie, dreams, memory, are simply different *modalities of experience*, none more 'inner' or 'outer' than any other" (p. 20). In our society, socialization creates a "split between experience and behavior" in which the inner is split from the outer (p. 54). *The Politics of Experience* (New York: Ballantine Books, 1967).

16. "The family's function is to repress Eros; to induce a false consciousness of security; to deny death by avoiding life; to cut off transcendence; to believe in God, not to experience the Void; to create, in short, *one dimensional man;* to promote respect, conformity, obedience; to con children out of play; to induce a fear of failure, to promote a respect for work; to promote a respect for 'respectability.' " *Ibid.*, p. 65.

17. For Freud, ". . . besides the instinct to preserve living substance and to pin it into ever larger units, there must exist another, contrary instinct seeking to dissolve those units and to bring them back to their primeval, inorganic state. That is to say, as well as Eros there was an instinct of death." *Civilization and Its Discontents* (New York: W. W. Norton, 1961), pp. 65–66, 92.

18. The Nazis taught Camus that the word "nihilism" cannot be used lightly; it has consequences. "What is truth, you used to ask? To be sure, but at least we know what falsehood is; that is just what you have taught us. What is spirit? We know its contrary, which is murder. What is man? There I stop you, for we know. Man

is that force which ultimately cancels all tyrants and gods. He is the force of evidence. Human evidence is what we must preserve, and our certainty at present comes from the fact that its fate and our country's fate are linked together. If nothing had any meaning, you would be right. But there is something that still has a meaning." Camus, "Letters to a German Friend: Second Letter," *Resistance, Rebellion and Death* (New York: Alfred A. Knopf, 1961), p. 14.

19. Camus, *The Myth of Sisyphus, op. cit.*, p. v.

20. Paul Hanly Furfey, *The Respectable Murderers: Social Evil and Christian Conscience* (New York: Herder & Herder, 1966), p. 160.

21. Richard Barnet, *Intervention and Revolution* (New York: New American Library, 1968).

22. Camus, *The Rebel* (New York: Random House, Vintage Books, 1956), p. 4.

23. In a critical survey of several hundred definitions of culture, A. L. Kroeber and Clyde Kluckholn concluded that most social scientists would accept the following: "Culture consists of patterns, explicit and implicit, of and for behavior acquired and transmitted by symbols, constituting the distinctive achievement of human groups, including their embodiment in artifacts; the essential core of culture consists of traditional (i.e., historically derived and selected) ideas and especially their attached values; culture systems may, on the one hand, be considered as products of action, on the other as conditioning elements of further action." *Culture* (New York: Random House, Vintage Books, 1952), p. 357.

24. See my "The Gap between Intellectuals and People," *A New Generation* (New York: Herder & Herder, 1964), and the profounder interpretation of the phenomena opened up by Robert N. Bellah's essay, "Civil Religion in America," with commentaries and a response in, *The Religious Situation: 1968*, ed. Donald R. Cutler (Boston: Beacon Press, 1968).

25. ". . . Behavioral scientists who believe themselves to be in possession of certain techniques of control and manipulation will tend to search for problems to which their knowledge and skills might be relevant, defining these as 'important problems.' " Noam Chomsky, "The Menace of Liberal Scholarship," *New York Review of Books*, 11, no. 12 (January 2, 1969): 29, 35. "Gide has said somewhere that he distrusts the carrying out of one possibility because it necessarily restricts other possibilities. Call the possibilities 'imaginative.' And call the carrying-out of *one* possibility the bureaucratization of the imaginative. An imaginative possibility . . . is bureaucratized when it is embodied in the realities of a social texture, in all the complexity of language and habits, in the property relationship, the method of government, production and distribution, and in the development of rituals that reinforce the same emphasis. . . . In the modern laboratory, the procedure of *invention* itself (the very essence of the imaginative) has been bureaucratized. . . . Science, knowledge, is the bureaucratization of wisdom." Kenneth Burke, *Attitudes Toward History* (Boston: Beacon Press, 1961), pp. 225–28.

26. ". . . there is an ethically sinister possibility in knowing the machinery of rules.

. . . In this sense, every sociologist is a potential saboteur or swindler, as well as a putative helpmate of oppression. . . . The social scientist shares this ethical predicament with his colleagues in the natural sciences, as the political use of nuclear physics has more than amply demonstrated in recent years. . . . As the physicists are busy engineering the world's annihilation, the social scientists can be entrusted with the smaller mission of engineering the world's consent." Peter Berger, *Invitation to Sociology: A Humanistic Perspective* (Garden City, N.Y.: Doubleday & Co., Anchor Books, 1963), p. 152. See also Chomsky, "Philosophers and Public Philosophy," *Ethics: An International Journal of Social, Political and Legal Philosophy* 79, no. 1 (October 1968): 1–9.

27. "The function of education has never been to free the mind and the spirit of man, but to bind them; and to the end that the mind and spirit of his children should never escape Homo sapiens has employed praise, ridicule, admonition, accusation, mutilation, and even torture to chain them to the cultural pattern. . . . American classrooms, like educational institutions anywhere, express the values . . . and fears found in the culture as a whole. School has no choice; . . [it] can give training in skills; it cannot teach creativity." Jules Henry, *Culture Against Man* (New York: Random House, Vintage Books, 1963), pp. 286–87; on American conformity in work, pp. 34–35. On political quiescence, see Murray Edelman, *The Symbolic Uses of Politics* (Chicago: University of Chicago Press, 1967), pp. 27–28, 32–33.

28. "Any well knit way of life molds human behavior into its own design. The individualism of bourgeois society like the communism of a socialized state must be inculcated from the nursery to the grave. In the United States, as one among the bourgeois nations, the life of personal achievement and personal responsibility is extolled in song and story from the very beginning of consciousness. Penny banks instill the habit of thrift; trading in the schoolyard propagates the bourgeois scale of values. Individual marks at school set the person at rivalrous odds with his fellows. 'Success and failure depend on you.' 'Strive and succeed' means 'If you strive, success comes; if success does not come, you have not striven hard enough.' When such an ideology impregnates life from start to finish, the thesis of collective responsibility runs against a wall of noncomprehension." Harold D. Lasswell, *Politics: Who Gets What, When, How?* (New York: Meridian Books, 1958), pp. 32–34.

29. Henry, *op. cit.*, pp. 27, 295–96.

30. "We could state the principle of the laboratory in this proposition: 'Every machine contains a cow-path.' That is: there are embodied somewhere in its parts . . . a process that remains simply because the originators of the machine embodied this process in their invention. It has been retained . . . because no one ever thought of questioning it. . . . As it stands, the process is a 'cow-path' in pious obedience to its secret grounding in the authority of custom." Burke, *op. cit.*, p. 228. "The state of having turbulent notions about things that seem to belong together, although in some unknown way, is a prescientific state, a sort of intellectual gestation period. This state the 'behavioral sciences' have sought to skip, hoping to learn its lessons by the way. . . . The result is that they have

modeled themselves on physics, which is not a suitable model. . . . The commitment to 'scientific method' could be seriously inimical to any advance of knowledge in such important but essentially humanistic pursuits [as the growing interrelationship of disciplines like psychology and biology]." Susanne Langer, *Mind: An Essay on Human Feeling* (Baltimore: Johns Hopkins Press, 1966), I:52–53.

31. "We prefer to deal with cases as they arise, 'on their merits'. . . . Pragmatism and bureaucracy thus combine to produce a diplomatic style marked by rigidity in advance of formal negotiations and excessive reliance on tactical considerations once negotiations start. . . . The overriding concern with tactics suppresses a feeling for nuance and for intangibles." Henry A. Kissinger, "The Vietnam Negotiations," *Foreign Affairs* 47, no. 2 (January 1969): 221–22.

32. Note how Kissinger's analysis accepts the basic presuppositions of American policy. For example, though he insists that decisions about "ultimate goals" cannot be avoided, he concludes: "However we got into Vietnam, whatever the judgment of our actions, ending the war honorably is essential for the peace of the world. Any other solution may unloose forces that would complicate prospects of international order." *Ibid.*, p. 234. It does not occur to him to question in whose interest that "order" might be, or how questionable the existent definition of that interest might be.

33. Edelman, *op. cit.*, pp. 74–75; Lasswell, *op, cit.*, pp. 168–71.

34. Lasswell, *op. cit.*, pp. 13–21, 172–73; Henry, *op. cit.*, pp. 3–44.

35. "Culture is the creation by man of a world of adjustment and meaning, in the context of which human life can be significantly lived." Thomas F. O'Dea, *The Sociology of Religion* (Englewood Cliffs, N.J.: Prentice-Hall, 1966), p. 3.

36. Richard B. Brandt, *Ethical Theory: The Problems of Normative and Critical Ethics* (Englewood Cliffs, N.J.: Prentice-Hall, 1959), pp. 4–10.

37. Contrast: "Our own body is the only thing in the world which we never experience as an object, but experience always in terms of the world to which we are attending from our body . . . it is not by looking at things, but by dwelling in them, that we understand their joint meaning, that is, their meaning *in relationship* with us." Michael Polanyi, *The Tacit Dimension* (Garden City, N.Y.: Doubleday & Co., 1966), pp. 16–18. See David B. Burrell, "Knowing as a Passionate and Personal Quest: C.S. Pierce," in *American Philosophy and the Future*, ed. Michael Novak (New York: Scribner's, 1968).

38. Morton White, *Toward Reunion in Philosophy* (Cambridge: Harvard University Press, 1956), pp. 222ff., 258ff., 279, 286–87.

39. Daniel Bell, in James Ridgeway, *The Closed Corporation: American Universities in Crisis* (New York: Random House, 1968), p. 3.

40. See Stuart Hampshire's discussion of intention in *Thought and Action* (New York: Viking Press, 1960), pp. 95–169.

41. ". . . Only those actions are properly called 'human' of which [a man] is master. . . . There are other acts that a man does, but because they are not man's simply as man, they may be called 'acts of man' but not strictly human acts." St. Thomas Aquinas, *Summa Theologica.* 1–2. 1.

42. See, e.g., Freud, *The Psychopathology of Everyday Life*, in *Basic Works of Freud* (New York: Modern Library, 1950), p. 139.

43. See Bernard Lonergan, S.J., *Collection*, ed. F. E. Crowe, S.J. (New York: Herder & Herder, 1967); also my *Belief and Unbelief* (New York: Macmillan Co., 1965), pp. 57–58; and my *Theology for Radical Politics, op. cit.* Compare "horizon" with the "field theory" of Henry Stack Sullivan, *The Interpersonal Theory of Psychiatry* (New York: W. W. Norton, 1953), pp. 367–68, 376, 381. For an anthology of recent sociological work on the role of society in shaping the self, see Bartlett H. Stoodley, *Society and Self* (Glencoe, Ill: Free Press, 1963).

44. "Durkheim's major concern in *Le Suicide* is with a society as collectivity, with the state of its *ordre collectif* and of its *conscience collective*. To describe Europe's collective consciousness pre-1900, Durkheim used the term *malaise*. A sickness, not economic but moral, he said, afflicts France and the West because all previously existing *cadres* have either broken down or been worn away by time. The family unit, its members dispersed and divorced, no longer exercises its old cohesive powers. Religion, through no fault of Science, is tossed aside by men who simply will not bow to the limits it places on conduct. The gravitational pull of political parties grows ever weaker, while the mutually binding and integrating demands on workers in the old *corporations des metiers* are binding no more. . . . Thus: social disorganization; discarded and discredited norms; a flat unwillingness to accept in any form a checkrein on pleasure, appetites, production or prosperity; this constellation of signs Durkheim translated into Greek. To the negative prefix *a* he added the plural of laws, *nomous*, and turned the 'no-laws' *anomous* into French as 'l'anomie.' " *Ibid.*, p. 235.

2. The Source of the Experience

1. See Berger, *op. cit.*, pp. 42–50.

2. "But social adaptation to a dysfunctional society may be dangerous. The perfectly adjusted bomber pilot may be a greater threat to species survival than the hospitalized schizophrenic deluded that the Bomb is inside him. Our society may itself have become biologically dysfunctional and some forms of schizophrenic alienation may have a socio-biological function that we have not recognized." Laing, *op. cit.*, p. 120.

3. "Intensive occupation with the more fully elaborated meaning systems available in our time gives one a truly frightening understanding of the way in which these systems can provide a total interpretation of reality, within which will be included an interpretation of the alternate systems and of the ways of passing from one system to another. . . . The meaning system [an individual] enters provides him with an interpretation of his existence and of his world, including in this interpretation an explanation of the meaning system he has abandoned. Also, the meaning system provides him with tools to combat his own doubts. Catholic confessional discipline, Communist 'autocriticism' and the psychoanalytic techniques of coping with 'resistance' all fulfill the same purpose of preventing

alternation out of the particular meaning system, allowing the individual to interpret his own doubts in terms derived from the system itself, thus keeping him within it." *Ibid.*, pp. 51–52.

4. "The primacy of the intellect lies . . . in a distant, distant future. . . . It will presumably set itself the same aims as those whose realization you expect from your God . . , namely the love of man and the decrease of suffering. . . . Our God, *Logos*, will fulfill whichever of these wishes nature outside us allows, but he will do it very gradually, only in the unforeseeable future, and for a new generation of men." Freud, *The Future of an Illusion* (New York: Doubleday & Co., Anchor Books, 1964), p. 88.

5. Replying to the view that existentialism is an encounter with nothingness, Charles Frankel says: "But nihilism as it is experienced . . . does not take a new theology or metaphysics to overcome it. It is the product of broken hopes, lost friends, impermanent commitments, and declining standards; and it may even be the symptom of a loss of intestinal fortitude." *Op. cit.*, p. 9.

6. Freud saw through the assumption when he said: "It may perhaps seem to you as though our theories are a kind of mythology. . . . But does not every science come in the end to a kind of mythology." "Why War?," *Collected Papers*, V:283; also see Polanyi, *op. cit.*

7. "In the general statement that constitutes the opening chapter of *Toward a General Theory of Action*, signed by Talcott Parsons, Edward A. Shils, Gordon W. Allport, Clyde Kluckhohn, Henry A. Murray, Robert R. Sears, Richard C. Sheldon, Samuel A. Stouffer, and Edward C. Tolman is found this affirmation: 'Some actors possess, to a high degree, the potentialities of elaborating their own goals and standards, accepting the content of institutional role-expectations but simultaneously modifying and adding something new to them. These are the creative personalities whose conformity or alienation is not mainly motivated by a need-disposition to accept or reject the given institutional role-expectations, but rather by the need to discover, elaborate, and conform with their own ego-ideal.' This is an admirable statement and gives notice of due attention to be paid to man the creator, although apparently the ability to transcend the clutch of culture is restricted to a few. What needs to be emphasized, however, is that this individual is nowhere to be found in the elaboration of this theoretical position, which has had so much impact on American sociology. Rather the stress is purely on the need-dispositions to conform or to deviate and upon the contradictions (sic) in institutional structure that have influence on such need-dispositions." William L. Kolb, "Images of Man and the Sociology of Religion," in Stoodley, *op. cit.*, pp. 633–34.

8. See, for example, *The Dissenting Academy*, ed. Theodore Roszak (New York: Random House, Pantheon Books, 1968); also, Chomsky, *American Power and the New Mandarins* (New York: Random House, Pantheon Books, 1968). Both books, however, seem to me too glib—oriented toward politics rather than toward culture.

9. To recapture the excitement of that time, possibly no text is more instructive than the lectures of William James at the Lowell Institute in Boston (1906) under

the title *Pragmatism* (New York: Washington Square Books, 1963).

10. Jacques Ellul, *The Technological Society* (New York: Random House, Vintage Books, 1967), pp. xxv, 5, 7–11, 19.

11. See Richard M. Jones, *Fantasy and Feeling in Education* (New York: New York University Press, 1968), pp. 4, 97.

12. Frankel, *The Case for Modern Man* (Boston: Beacon Press, 1964), and his *The Love of Anxiety, op. cit.*

13. For a clearly drawn debate on this issue, see Zbigniew Brzezinski, "Revolution and Counterrevolution," in *The New Republic*, 158, no. 22 (June 1, 1968); and Arthur P. Mendel, "Robots and Rebels," *The New Republic* 160, no. 2 (January 11, 1969); *The Dissenting Academy, op. cit.;* Paul Goodman, *Compulsory Miseducation* (New York: Random House, Vintage Books 1964). For more cautious criticism see Christopher Jencks and David Riesman, *The Academic Revolution* (Garden City, N.Y.: Doubleday & Co., 1968), chaps. 5, 12.

14. Frankel's response to such critics is brave: "We can explain a given event by placing it in a system of laws. When asked why these laws are as they are, we can answer by connecting them with a more embracing system of laws. And we can go on and on, but at some point we are going to have to stop and say that we know no more, that we have gone as far as, at the moment, we can go. This is a position which is in thorough accord with that of modern empirical rationalism. The difference is only that the irrationalist describes this state of affairs as a 'primal mystery.' But why should he do so? All that has been shown is that no matter what explanation we give of events, no matter how we answer the question Why? it is always possible to ask for a further explanation. If the irrationalist finds this fact about human knowledge a primal mystery, this reveals that he continues to think that the ideal of absolute, infallible, and final knowledge makes sense. He is, in other words, a philosophical rationalist in the pure Platonic sense of the term—a philosophical rationalist *manqué*. The believers in human reason whom the irrationalist attacks for their *hubris* do not make the demands on human intelligence that he does—which is why they do not announce that their hearts are broken by the discovery of 'human finitude.'" *Op. cit.*, p. 32. It is not Plato but a world shaped by "modern empirical rationalism" that today makes some men anxious and breaks some men's hearts.

15. See Polanyi, *Personal Knowledge* (Chicago: University of Chicago Press, 1958), and his *Tacit Dimension, op. cit.;* Ernest G. Schachtel, *Metamorphosis: On the Development of Affect, Perception, Attention, and Memory* (New York: Basic Books, 1959), p. 171.

16. Frankel, *The Love of Anxiety, op. cit.*, pp. 24–25.

17. James Watson, *The Double Helix* (New York: Atheneum, 1968). See, e.g., Loren Eiseley, *The Unexpected Universe* (New York: Harcourt, Brace & World, 1969).

18. Goodman, *Growing Up Absurd* (New York: Random House, Vintage Books, 1962); Edgar Friedenberg, *Coming of Age in America* (New York: Random House, Vintage Books, 1963); Schachtel, "On Memory and Childhood Amnesia," in *op. cit.*, pp. 279–322.

19. "Millions of processes—the whole dynamic rounds of metabolism, digestion,

circulation and endocrine action—are normally not felt. One may say that some activities, especially nervous ones, above a certain (probably fluctuating) limen of intensity, enter into 'physical phase.' This is the phase of being felt. It may develop suddenly, with great distinctness of quality, location and value-character, for instance, in response to a painful stimulus; or similarly, only with less precise location in the organism, like a shock of terror; or a deeply engendered process may go gradually, perhaps barely, into a physical phase of vague awareness—come and gone— a sense of wariness or a fleeting emotive moment. The normal substrate of 'feeling-tone,' from which the more acute tensions build up into specific experiences, is probably a dynamic pattern of nervous activities playing freely across the limen of sentience.

"It is this transiency and general ability of the psychical phase that accounts for the importance of preconscious processes in the construction of such elaborate phenomena as ideas, intentions, images and fantasies, and makes it not only reasonable but obvious that they are rooted in the fabric of totally unfelt activities. . . ." Susanne Langer, *op. cit.*, p. 22.

20. See my *A Theology for Radical Politics, op. cit.*, pp. 88–90.

21. Werner Heisenberg, "The Representation of Nature in Contemporary Physics," in *Symbolism in Religion and Literature*, ed. Rollo May (New York: George Braziller, 1959), pp. 226–27.

22. *Ibid.*

23. "From the time and capital that must be committed, the inflexibility of this commitment, the needs of large organization and the problems of market performance under conditions of advanced technology, comes the necessity for planning. Tasks must be performed so that they are right not for the present but for that time in the future when, companion and related work having also been done, the whole job is completed. And the amount of capital that, meanwhile, will have been committed adds urgency to this need to be right. So conditions at the time of completion of the whole task must be foreseen as must developments along the way. And steps must be taken to prevent, offset or otherwise neutralize the effect of adverse developments, and to insure that what is ultimately foreseen eventuates in fact." John Kenneth Galbraith, *The New Industrial State* (Boston: Houghton Mifflin Co., 1967), p. 16. Also see Michael Harrington, *Towards a Democratic Left* (New York: Macmillan Co., 1968).

24. Eldridge Cleaver, *Soul on Ice* (New York: McGraw-Hill, 1967), pp. 192–204.

25. Speculating on a potential new myth of the "machinehood of humanity," Lasswell declares: "In the latest stages of urban civilization man has nurtured the means of his own supercession and fulfillment. He has created an object . . . in the image of his highest aspirations. Man may subside into a fossil, living or dead; at least he will have performed an unprecendented role of midwifery in cosmic evolution. . . . Many of the newly ascendant elite may be in no mood to celebrate their historical dependence upon human life . . . [which] may lead to a counter-myth that relegates man to an inferior caste position in the new cosmic order." *World Politics and Personal Insecurity* (New York: Free Press, 1965), p. x.

26. See Lonergan, *Insight, op. cit.*
27. See Kroeber and Kluckhohn, *op. cit.*, pp. 362–64.
28. See Richard M. Jones's discussion of the work of Herbert Silberer in elucidating certain preconscious forms of inspiration: "... *'apperceptive insufficiency'* refers to situations in which a person is at the top of his form, in full command of his optimal mental state, but who has momentarily assumed challenges which just barely elude his best intellectual efforts. He may then receive an assist from these same prerationative approximations. We sometimes call this 'inspiration.'" *Op. cit.*, p. 66.
29. "It was Freud's most significant contribution to our understanding of ourselves that common sense misleads us in this matter, that in fact we alter the world, change it, play with it, make it up and over constantly, when awake and asleep, in every perceptual, cognitive, and recognitive event, whether extraceptively framed or intraceptively framed.... we school our children the better that they may develop their distinctly human capacity to condition their stimuli. That is, to use their imaginations, and thus to contribute to their culture." *Ibid.*, pp. 59, 61.
30. See Julian Huxley, *Evolution in Action* (New York: Harper & Row, 1963). Kroeber and Kluckhohn quote anthropologist Murdock approvingly: "... social organization is a semi-independent system comparable in many respects to language, and similarly characterized by an internal dynamics of its own ... it demonstrably does change in response to external events, and in identifiable ways. Nevertheless, its own structure appears to act as a filter for the influences which affect it." *Op Cit.*, pp. 361–62n, 49.
31. Jones, *op. cit.*, pp. 70–71,77; Freud, "The Uncanny," in *On Creativity and the Unconscious* (New York: Harper & Bros., Harper Torchbooks, 1958), pp. 122–61.
32. Martin Heidegger, *Being and Time*, trans. J. Macquarrie and E. Robinson (New York: Harper & Row, 1962), div. 2, sect. 50, p. 295.
33. John S. Dunne, *The City of the Gods: A Study in Myth and Mortality* (New York: Macmillan Co., 1965).
34. Erik Erikson has drawn an epigenetic chart of the emotional growth of the person from infancy to maturity. He distinguishes eight psychosocial stages in the life cycle and eight corresponding "nuclear conflicts" that, if resolved in a healthy manner, produce strengths that aid the person in coping with the next stage:

I. Oral Sensory—Basic Trust vs. Mistrust—Drive and Hope.

II. Muscular-Anal—Autonomy vs. Shame, Doubt—Self Control and Willpower.

III. Locomotor-Genital—Initiative vs. Guilt—Direction and Purpose.

IV. Latency—Industry vs. Inferiority—Method and Competence.

V. Puberty and Adolescence—Identity vs. Role Confusion—Devotion and Fidelity.

VI. Young Adulthood—Intimacy vs. Isolation—Affiliation and Love.

VII. Adulthood—Generativity vs. Stagnation—Production and Care.

VIII. Maturity—Ego Integrity vs. Despair—Renunciation and Wisdom.

Childhood and Society, rev. & enlarged ed. (New York: W. W. Norton, 1963), pp. 273–74.

35. See, e.g., Gilbert Ryle, *The Concept of Mind* (New York: Barnes & Noble, 1960).

36. See Jacques Maritain, *Creative Intuition in Art and Poetry* (New York: Meridian Books, 1955), pp. 51–75.

37. Lawrence Kubie, "Research in Protecting Preconscious Functions in Education," *Contemporary Educational Psychology: Selected Essays*, ed. Richard M. Jones (New York: Harper & Row, 1967), pp. 76–78.

38. "Nothing, nothing had the least importance, and I knew quite well why. . . . What difference could they make to me, the deaths of others, or a mother's love, or his God; or the way a man decides to live, the fate he thinks he chooses, since one and the same fate was bound to 'choose' not only me but thousands of millions of privileged people who, like him, called themselves my brothers. Surely, surely he must see that? Every man alive was privileged; there was only one class of men, the privileged class. All alike would be condemned to die one day; his turn, too, would come like the others'. And what difference could it make if, after being charged with murder, he were executed because he didn't weep at his mother's funeral, since it all came to the same thing in the end?" Camus, *The Stranger*, (New York: Random House, Vintage Books, 1961), p. 152.

39. Camus, *The Myth of Sisyphus, op. cit.*, p. 5.

40. Camus, *The Rebel, op. cit.*, p. 4.

41. "Yes, the old fellow had been right; these people were 'just the same as ever.' But this was at once their strength and their innocence, and it was on this level, beyond all grief, that Rieux could feel himself at one with them. . . . Dr. Rieux resolved to compile this chronicle . . . ; so that some memorial of the injustice and outrage done them might endure; and to state quite simply what we learn in a time of pestilence: that there are more things to admire in men than to despise. Nonetheless . . . the tale . . . could not be one of final victory. It could be only the record of what had had to be done . . . in the never ending fight against terror and its relentless onslaughts, despite their personal afflictions, by all who, while unable to be saints but refusing to bow down to pestilences, strive their utmost to be healers." Camus, *The Plague* (New York: Modern Library, 1948), p. 278.

42. Sartre, "Existentialism," *Existentialism and Human Emotions, op. cit.*, pp. 26–35.

43. "We were never more free than during the German occupation. We had lost . . . all our rights, beginning with the right to talk. Every day we were insulted to our faces and had to take it in silence. Under one pretext or another, as workers, Jews, or political prisoners, we were deported *en masse*. Everywhere, on billboards, in the newspapers, on the screen, we encountered the revolting and insipid picture of ourselves that our suppressors wanted us to accept. And because of all this we were free. Because the Nazi venom seeped into our thought, every accurate thought was a conquest . . . exile, captivity, and especially death (which we usually shrink from facing at all in happier days) became for us the habitual objects of our concern. We learned that they were

neither inevitable accidents, nor even constant and inevitable dangers, but they must be considered as our lot itself, our destiny, the profound source of our reality as men." Sartre, in William Barrett, *Irrational Man* (New York: Doubleday & Co., Anchor Books, 1962), pp. 239–40.

44. Nietzsche, *op. cit.*, p. 7.

45. "My reasoning wants to be faithful to the evidence that aroused it. That evidence is the absurd. It is that divorce between the mind that desires and the world that disappoints, my nostalgia for unity, this fragmented universe and the contradiction that binds them together." Camus, *The Myth of Sisyphus, op. cit.*, p. 37.

46. Sartre, "Existentialism," *op. cit.*, pp. 44–47.

47. Immanuel Kant, *The Philosophy of Kant* (New York: Modern Library, 1949), pp. 132–39.

48. See lengthy passage quoted from William James later in this chapter.

49. Peter Caws, "What is Structuralism," *Partisan Review*, winter 1968, p. 82.

50. Erikson defines the ego as "the domain of an inner 'agency' safeguarding our coherent existence by screening and synthesizing, in any series of moments, all the impressions, emotions, memories, and impulses which try to enter our thought and demand our action, and which would tear us apart if unsorted and unmanaged by a slowly grown and reliably watchful screening system." He adds: "Members of the same species and of other species are always part of each other's *Umwelt*. By the same token, then, and accepting the fact that the human environment is social, *the outerworld of the ego* is made up of the *egos of others* significant to it. They are significant because on many levels of crude or subtle communication my whole being perceives in them a hospitality for the way in which my inner world is ordered and includes them, which makes me, in turn, hospitable to the way they order their world and include me—a mutual affirmation, then, which can be depended upon to activate my being as I can be depended upon to activate theirs." *Identity: Youth and Crisis*, (New York: W. W. Norton, 1968), pp. 218–19.

51. See Sartre, "Existentialism," *op. cit.*, pp. 41f.

52. See *The Writings of William James*, ed. John J. McDermott (New York: Random House, 1967), p. 6.

53. "Madness has become man's possibility of absolving both man and the world— and even those images . . . that challenge the world and deform man. It is, far beyond dreams, beyond the nightmare of bestiality, the last recourse: the end and the beginning of everything . ., but because it is the ambiguity of chaos and apocalypse: Goya's *Idiot* who shrieks and twists his shoulder to escape from the nothingness that imprisons him—is this the birth of the first man and his first movement toward liberty, or the last convulsion of the last dying man?

"And this madness that links and divides time, that twists the world into the ring of a single night, this madness so foreign to the experience of its contemporaries, does it not transmit—to those able to receive it, to Nietzsche and to Artaud—those barely audible voices of classical unreason, in which it was always a question of nothingness and night, but amplifying them now to shrieks

131

and frenzy? But giving them for the first time an expression, a *droit de cité*, and a hold on Western culture which makes possible all contestations, as well as *total* contestation? But restoring their primitive savagery?" Michel Foucault, *Madness and Civilization: A History of Insanity in the Age of Reason* (New York: New American Library, Mentor Books, 1967), pp. 225–26. See also Claude Levi-Strauss, *Totemism* (Boston: Beacon Press, 1967), p. 2.

54. *The Writings of William James, op. cit.*, p. 7.

55. *Ibid.*, pp. 7–8.

56. ". . . historical processes have already entered the individual's core in childhood. Past history survives in the ideal and evil prototypes which guide the parental imagery and which color fairy tale and family lore, superstition and gossip, and the simple lessons of early verbal training. Historians on the whole make little of this; they account only for the contest of autonomous historical ideas and are unconcerned with the fact that these ideas reach down into the lives of generations and re-emerge through the daily awakening and training of historical consciousness in young individuals: via the mythmakers of religion and politics, of the arts and the sciences, of drama, cinema and fiction—all contributing more or less consciously, more or less responsibly to the historical logic absorbed by youth. And today we must add to these, at least in the United States, psychiatry and the social sciences, and all over the world, the press, which force all significant behavior into the open and add immediate reportorial distortion and editorial response." Erikson, *Identity, op. cit.*, p. 257. See also Sullivan, *op. cit.* pp. 382–84.

Again, "Every culture is also a structure of expectancies. If we know a culture, we know what various classes of individuals within it expect from each other —and from outsiders of various categories. We know what types of activity are held to be inherently gratifying." Kluckhohn, *Culture and Behavior* (New York: Free Press, 1965), p. 69.

Some sociologists have begun to discuss the connection between ethics and cultural orders, insisting at the outset, that they are not identical. Cf. Gertrude Jaeger and Philip Selznick: "Moral enlightenment often depends upon the weakening of symbols, upon making profane what was formerly sacred, upon taking people for what they are and not for their symbolic status and value. . . . On the other hand, a moral order may be weak and precarious if it does not produce cultural symbols, and is not sustained by them." "A Normative Theory of Culture," *American Sociological Review* 29, no. 5 (October 1964): 666–67.

57. "The statement that the human infant is born preadapted to an 'average expectable environment' implies a more truly biological as well as an inescapably societal formulation. For not even the very best of mother-child relationships could, by themselves, account for that subtle and complex 'milieu' which permits a human baby not only to survive but also to develop his potentialities for growth and uniqueness. Man's ecology demands constant natural, historical, and technological readjustment, which makes it at once obvious that only a perpetual, if ever so imperceptible, restructuring of tradition can safeguard for each new

generation of infants anything approaching an 'average expectability' of environment. . . .

"The specific kind of preadaptedness of the human infant—namely, the readiness to grow by epigenetic steps through psychosocial crises—calls not only for one basic environment, but for a whole sequence of 'expectable' environments, for as the child adapts in spurts and stages he has a claim, at any given stage reached, to the next 'average expectable environment.' In other words, the human environment as a whole must permit and safeguard a series of more or less discontinuous and yet culturally and psychologically consistent developments, each extending further along the radius of expanding life tasks. All of this makes man's so-called biological adaptation a matter of life cycles developing within their community's changing history." Erikson, *Identity, op. cit.*, pp. 222–23. See also his *Childhood and Society, op. cit.*, pp. 247–51.

58. Berger, *op. cit.*, pp. 54–65. See also Robert Jay Lifton, "Protean Man," *Partisan Review, op. cit.*, pp. 13–34.

3. Inventing the Self

1. *Ascent of Mount Carmel*, trans. E. Allison Peers (Garden City, N.Y.: Doubleday & Co., Image Books, 1958), p. 72.
2. Paul Tillich, *The Courage to Be* (New Haven: Yale University Press, 1963).
3. Edmund Stillman and William Pfaff, *The Politcs of Hysteria* (London: V. Gollancz, 1964), "The Two Faces of Western Man," esp. pp. 16–22.
4. Foucault, *op. cit.*
5. Kubie, in Richard M. Jones, *An Application of Psychoanalysis to Education* (Springfield, Ill.: Charles C. Thomas, 1960), p. viii; quoted in *Feeling and Fantasy in Education, op. cit.*, p. 126.
6. See Karl Rahner, "On the Question of a Formal Existential Ethics," *Theological Investigations* (Baltimore: Helicon, 1963), II: 217–34.
7. Sartre, *Being and Nothingness, op. cit.*, pp. 56–89.
8. Pierre Aubenque, "La Source Tragique," *La Prudence d'Aristotle* (Paris: Presses universitaires de France, 1962), pp. 71–93.
9. Werner Jaeger, *Aristotle: Fundamentals of the History of His Development*, trans. Richard Robinson (New York: Oxford University Press, 1962); Aubenque, *op. cit.*, pp. 64–105, and "Etre et histoire," *Le Problem de l'être chez Aristotle* (Paris: Presses universitaires de France, 1962), pp. 71–93. The role of fortune and chance in the *Physics* should not be overlooked; Aristotle defines "nature" not as what happens necessarily but only as what happens with statistical regularity; see *Physics*, trans. Rev. P. Wicksteed and F.M. Cornford (Cambridge: Harvard University Press), II, chaps. 1, 2, 5, 6.
10. See H. Rommen, *The Natural Law* (St. Louis: B. Herder, 1959).
11. On Aristotle's break with Plato's conception of ethics see Jaeger, *op. cit.* Jaeger's thesis has been much disputed—the literature evaluating it is enormous—but his

central point seems to stand firm; see also *Nicomachean Ethics*, rev. ed., trans. H. Rackham (Cambridge: Harvard University Press, 1934), I.vi.i.

12. Where "dialectical" means search for inner contradictions between manifest and latent aims.

13. Bernard Lonergan, S. J., *The Subject* (Milwaukee: Marquette University Press, 1968), p. 25.

14. See Rackham's note: "Morally inferior people like things that are only pleasant 'accidentally,' i.e. owing not to some quality inherent in the thing but to something extraneous to it . . . the same person thinks the same thing pleasant at one time and unpleasant at another—and so repents today of his indulgence yesterday; or he desires two incompatible things at once, or desires a thing with one part of his nature that he dislikes with another, so that there is a conflict between his desires, or between his desire for pleasure and his wish for what he thinks good. . . ." *Ethics, op.cit.*, I.viii.11. Aristotle dwells on this relation between pleasure and nobility of soul when he discusses genuine self-love and friendship, *ibid.*, IX.iv.5–10. His key point is: "Things pleasant by nature are pleasant to lovers of what is noble, and so also are actions. . . . Therefore their life has no need of pleasure as a sort of ornamental appendage." *Ibid.*, I.viii.11–12. Contrast with Rackham's note: "For the good man is of one mind with himself, and desires the same things with every part of his nature. Also, he wishes his own good, real as well as apparent, and seeks it by action (for it is a mark of a good man to exert himself actively for the good). . . ." *Ibid.*, IX.iv.3.

15. "It follows that the Good of man is the active exercise of his soul's faculties in conformity with excellence or virtue . . . Moreover, this activity must occupy a complete lifetime." *Ibid.*, I.vii.15–16.

16. ". . . the generality of men and the most vulgar identify the good with pleasure and accordingly are content with the life of enjoyment. For there are three specially prominent styles of life, the life of enjoyment, the life of politics, and thirdly the life of contemplation. The generality of mankind then show themselves to be utterly slavish, by preferring what is only a life for cows; but they get a hearing for their view as reasonable because many persons of high position share it." *Ibid.*, I.v.1–3. [I have modified the translation slightly, for clarity]; ". . . great and frequent reverses can crush and mar our bliss both by the pain they cause and by the hindrance they offer to many activities. Yet nevertheless even in adversity nobility shines through. . . ." *Ibid.*, I.x.12; ". . . of Courage, the death or wounds that it may bring will be painful to the courageous man . . ; but he will endure them because it is noble to do so, or . . . it is base not to do so. . . . It is not true therefore of every virtue that its active exercise is essentially pleasant, save in so far as it attains its end." *Ibid.* III.ix.4–5.

17. In a footnote to the word "Happiness" the translator notes: "This translation of ευδαιμονια can hardly be avoided, but it would perhaps be more accurately rendered by 'Well-being' or 'Prosperity'; and it will be found that the writer does not interpret it as a state of feeling but as a kind of activity." *Ibid.*, I.iv.2a.

18. For example: "We may arrive at a definition of Prudence by considering who are the persons we call prudent." *Ibid.*, VI.v.i.; "Hence men like Pericles are deemed

prudent, because they possess a faculty of discerning what things are good for themselves and for mankind; and that is our conception of an expert in Domestic Economy or Political Science." *Ibid.*, VI.v.5.

19. "Moreover, it is not easy to see *how* knowing that same Ideal Good will help a weaver or carpenter in the practice of his own craft. . . . In fact it does not appear that the physician studies even health in the abstract; . . . it is individuals he has to cure." *Ibid.*, I.vi.16; The notion of mean "relative to us" is also intended to account for differences from individual to individual: "Suppose that 10 pounds of food is a large ration for anybody and 2 pounds a small one: it does not follow that a trainer will prescribe 6 pounds for perhaps even this will be a large ration, or a small one, for the particular athlete." *Ibid.*, II.vi.7–8.

20. "The whole theory of conduct is bound to be an outline only and not an exact system. . . . Matters of conduct and expediency have nothing fixed or invariable about them, any more than have matters of health. And if this is true of the general theory of ethics, still less is exact precision possible in . . . particular cases of conduct; . . . the agents themselves have to consider what is suited to the circumstances on each occasion, just as in the case . . . of medicine or of navigation." *Ibid.*, II.ii.3–5; see also I.xi.2–3; and VI.v.3 and *passim*.

21. Burke, *Grammar of Motives* (New York: George Braziller, 1955), pp. 39, 242.

22. "Stated broadly the dialectical (agonistic) approach to knowledge is through the *act* of assertion, whereby one 'suffers' the kind of knowledge that is the reciprocal of his act. This is the process embodied in tragedy, where the agent's action involves a corresponding passion, and from the sufferance of the passion there arises an understanding of the act, and understanding that transcends the act. The act, in being an assertion, has called forth a counter-assertion in the elements that compose its context. And when the agent is enabled to see in terms of this counter-assertion, he has transcended the state that characterized him at the start. In this final state of tragic vision, intrinsic and extrinsic motivations are merged. That is, although purely circumstantial factors participate in his tragic destiny, these are not felt as exclusively external, or scenic; for they bring about a *representative* kind of accident, the kind of accident that belongs with the agent's particular kind of character." *Ibid.*, pp. 38–40.

23. "All cultures constitute so many somewhat distinct answers to essentially the same questions posed by human biology and by the generalities of the human situation." Kroeber and Kluckhohn, *op. cit.*, p. 348.

24. "Whether we are trained from childhood . . . is . . . of supreme importance." *Ethics, op. cit.*, II.i.8ff; "In fact pleasures and pains are the things with which moral virtue is concerned. For pleasure causes us to do base actions and pain causes us to abstain from doing noble actions. Hence the importance. . . . of having been definitely trained from childhood to like and dislike the proper things; this is what good education means." *Ibid.*, II.iii.2; "Men are corrupted through pleasures and pains." *Ibid.*, II.iii.5.

25. "We must therefore by some means secure that the character shall have at the outset a natural affinity for virtue, loving what is noble and hating what is base. And it is difficult to obtain a right education in virtue, from youth up without

being brought up under right laws; for to live temperately and hardily is not pleasant to most men, especially when young." *Ibid.*, X.ix.8; also, X.ix.11.

26. "[Virtue] . . . can be attained by some process of study or effort by all persons whose capacity for virtue has not been stunted or maimed." *Ibid.*, I.ix.4–5; "and so with infirmities and mutilations . . . nobody would reproach, but rather pity, a person blind from birth, or owing to disease or accident." *Ibid.*, III.v.15.

27. "A man needs to be born with moral vision, so to speak, whereby to discern correctly and choose what is truly good. A man of good natural disposition is a man well endowed by nature in this respect; [this is] . . . the greatest and noblest of gifts, . . . it has been bestowed on him at birth." *Ibid.*, III.v.17–19; but Aristotle, although he entertains this view as partially true, characteristically stresses that "our characters are the result of our conduct," *ibid.*, 10–14. cf. *ibid.*, X.ix.6–10, and Erikson, *Insight and Responsibility, op. cit.*, p. 69.

28. "A voluntary act would seem to be an act of which the origin lies in the agent, who knows the particular circumstances in which he is acting." *Ethics, op. cit.*, III.i.20–21. ". . . men are themselves responsible for having become careless through living carelessly . . . they acquire a particular quality by constantly acting in a particular way. This is shown by the way in which men train themselves for some contest or pursuit: they practice continually." *Ibid.*, III.v.10–11; "If the choice is to be good, both the principle must be true and the desire right, and that desire must pursue the same things as principle affirms." *Ibid.*, VI.ii.2–3. "Now it is held to be the mark of a prudent man to be able to deliberate well about what is good and advantageous for himself, . . . as a means to the good life in general." *Ibid.*, VI.vii.7.

29. ". . . it is right to feel anger at some things, and also to feel desire for some things, for instance health, knowledge. . . . the irrational feelings are just as much a part of human nature as the reason." *Ibid.*, III.i.24–27; ". . . the seat of the appetites and of desire in general does in a sense participate in principle, as being amenable and obedient to it (in the sense in fact in which we speak of 'paying heed' to one's father and friends. . .)." *Ibid.*, I.xiii,18; "It is by the practical experience of life and conduct that the truth is really tested, since it is there that the final decision lies." *Ibid.*, X.viii.12; see also remarks on the enjoyment of noble action *Ibid.*, I.viii.12; IX.iv.5–10.

30. "In the case of each of the moral qualities or dispositions [and virtues] . . . there is a certain mark to aim at on which the man who knows the principle involved fixes his gaze." *Ibid.*, VI.i.1; "Virtue has the quality of hitting the mean. . . . For example, one can feel desire or anger or pity . . ; whereas to feel these feelings at the right time, on the right occasion, towards the right people, for the right purpose and in the right manner, is to feel the best amount of them . . . and . . . the mark of virtue." *Ibid.*, II.vi.9–11.

31. *Ibid.*, II.vi.14; ix.2.

32. Aristotle has not clearly differentiated "will" from other desires. See C. J. O'Neil, "The Aristotelian Prudent Man," in *Imprudence in St. Thomas Aquinas* (Milwaukee: Marquette University Press, 1955).

33. The failure to make this distinction thus causes him serious difficulties in his

theory of moral weakness or *akrasia*. See J. J. Walsh, *Aristotle's Conception of Moral Weakness* (New York: Columbia University Press, 1963). The emphasis on the passage from insight to action, however, is unmistakable: ". . . in the practical sciences the end is not to attain a theoretic knowledge of the various subjects, but rather to carry out our theories in action." *Ethics, op. cit.*, X.ix.1.

34. Jaeger, *Paideia, op. cit.*, pp. xxvi, 278, 316–18; Burke, *Grammar of Motives, op. cit.*, p. 253–54.

35. "Yet to what degree and how seriously a man must err to be blamed is not easy to determine on principle. For in fact no object of perception is easy to define; and such questions of degree depend on particular circumstances." *Ethics, op. cit.*, II.ix.8.

36. Aristotle notes that if it could be taught by general principles, then anyone wishing to make "other people better by discipline" would presumably have to acquire the "science of legislation," but he notes wryly: ". . . nor yet do we notice that they [experts on legislation—politicians] have made their own sons or any others of their friends into statesmen." *Ibid.*, X.ix.18; "We do not see men becoming expert physicians from a study of medical handbooks." *Ibid.*, 21.

37. ἐν τῇ αἰσθήσει ἡ κρίσις". . . the decision lies with perception." *Ibid.*, II.ix.8.

38. "Hence choice may be called either thought related to desire or desire related to thought; and man, as an originator of action, is a union of desire and intellect." *Ibid.*, VI.ii.5. The translator notes that Aristotle views the word (choice) "as directed to means" *and* "to the selection of ends. . . . it is almost equivalent to purpose." *Ibid.*, III.ii.1a.

39. *Ibid.*, II.vi.14–15.

40. *Ibid.*, III.iv.4.

41. *Ibid.*, III.iv.4–5.

42. The first sentence of the *Ethics* declares: "Every art and every investigation and likewise every practical pursuit or undertaking, seems to aim at some good: hence it has been well said that the Good is that at which all things aim." *Ibid.*, I.i.1. The chapter warns us that "good" has several senses; not all things taken to be good are ethically good. The argument is not logical but dialectical.

43. *Ibid.*, III.iv.5–6.

44. "If . . . the means to our end are matters of deliberation and choice, it follows that actions dealing with these means are done by choice and are voluntary . . . virtues depend on our selves . . . we are free to act . . . [and] free to refrain from acting . . ; if therefore we are responsible . . . [and] it is in our power to do . . . right and wrong, it consequently depends on us whether we are virtuous or vicious." *Ibid.*, III.v.1–3.

45. Aristotle does propose three working rules: (a) Faced with opposing tendencies, steer nearest the least evil, pulling the vector of the outcome in that direction; do not merely take the mediocre midpoint between them. (b) Note the errors which blow you off course, then lean hard against the wind. (c) Note what you do when surprised, especially by pleasure or by pain, and count that a true index of your present development. Keep special watch on what gives you pleasure, not because evil but because deceptive. *Ibid.*, II.ix.3–6.

46. *Ibid.*, II.ix.7.
47. *Ibid.*, II.ix.4.
48. *Ibid.*, II.ix.7.
49. *Ibid.*
50. ". . . the end of this science is not knowledge but action." *Ibid.*, I.iii.6. ". . . our present study, unlike the other branches of philosophy, has a practical aim (for we are not investigating the nature of virtue for the sake of knowing what it is, but in order that we may become good, without which result our investigation would be of no use . . .)." *Ibid.*, II.ii.1.
51. See the translation of this phrase in *Introduction to Aristotle*, ed. Richard McKeon (New York: Modern Library, 1947), p. 538 (Book X.ix.5.).
52. "Hence the common remark about a perfect work of art, that you could not take from it nor add to it—meaning that excess and deficiency destroy perfection, while adherence to the mean preserves it—if then, as we say, good craftsmen look to the mean, and if virtue, like nature, is more accurate and better than any form of art, it will follow that virtue has the quality of hitting the mean." *Ibid.*, II.vi.9–10.
53. As an example of what he means by observing the mean in courage, Aristotle says: "For even in athletic contests it is not the bravest men who are the best fighters, but those who are strongest and in the best training." *Ibid.*, III.viii.8; see also *ibid.*, III.ix.3–4.
54. *Ibid.*, VI.i.1; I.ii.2.
55. "Prudence is indeed the same quality of mind as Political Science, though their essence is different." *Ibid.*, VI.viii.1–2; "Yet probably a man cannot pursue his own welfare without Domestic Economy and even Politics." *Ibid.*, VI.viii.4; ". . . [the science of Politics] lays down laws as to what people shall do, . . . the end of this science must include the ends of all the others. Therefore the Good of man must be the end of . . . Politics . . . The Good of the state is . . . greater and more perfect [than the good of the individual]. . . . Our investigation is in a sense the study of Politics." *Ibid.*, I.ii.7–8.
56. For contrasting presentations of one or other of these points: E.Barker, *The Political Thought of Plato and Aristotle* (New York: Dover Publications, 1959), and Abraham Edel, *Aristotle* (New York: Dell, 1967). See G.R.G. Mure, *Aristotle* (New York: Oxford University Press, Galaxy Books, 1964), for a supporting view.
57. *Not* "between."
58. "In point of excellence and rightness it [the mean] is an extreme." *Ethics, op. cit.*, II.vi.17; see also *ibid.*, 20, and *ibid.*, ix.9.
59. "Hence choice may be called either thought related to desire or desire related to thought; and man, as an originator of action, is a union of desire and intellect." *Ibid.*, VI.ii.5.
60. John Herman Randall, Jr., *Aristotle* (New York: Columbia University Press, 1963), p. 258.
61. But see his reflections on death and terror, in Book III. For example, in speaking of the courageous man, he notes that such a man would be afraid of some things:

". . . there are some terrors which we pronounce beyond human endurance, and these of course are fearful to everyone in this sense." *Ethics, op. cit.*, III.vii.1. Although he argues that a man who does not enjoy noble actions is not really a good man (I.viii.12), he understands that the courageous man must endure so much pain that his pleasure is "obscured." "This is illustrated by the case of athletic contests: to boxers, for example, their end—the object they box for . . . —is pleasant, but the blows they receive must hurt them. . . ; and these painful incidents are so numerous that the final object . . . appears not to contain any pleasure at all. If then the same is true of Courage, the death or wounds that it may bring will be painful to the courageous man and he will suffer them unwillingly; but he will endure them because it is noble to do so. . . . And the more a man possesses all virtue, and the more happy he is, the more pain death will cause him; for to such a man life is worth most, and he stands to lose the greatest goods, and knows that this is so, and this must be painful. But he is nonetheless courageous." *Ibid.*, III.ix.3–4.

62. For the systematic critique of the differences, see Lonergan, *Insight, op. cit.*, pp. 407, 408, 466–67, and his *Collection, op. cit.*, pp.142–51.

63. Karl Barth, "The Command of God," in *Church Dogmatics* (Edinburgh: T & T. Clark, 1957), II, part 2, pp. 509–781; Emil Brunner, *The Divine Imperative* (Philadelphia: Westminster Press, 1957).

64. Kant, *Fundamental Principles of the Metaphysic of Morals* (New York: Liberal Arts Press, 1949); R. M. Hare, *The Language of Morals* (London: Oxford University Press, 1961).

65. Søren Kierkegaard, *Sickness Unto Death* (Garden City, N.Y.: Doubleday & Co., 1954).

66. See Lasswell, *World Politics, op. cit.*, pp. 202–12.

67. Rieff, *op. cit.*, pp. 242, 246, 252–53, 255, 260.

68. To feel is to be acting; it is a horizon in act: "The fact that we can call something by a name, such as 'Feeling,' makes it seem like a kind of thing, an ingredient in nature or a product. But 'Feel' is a verb, and to say that what is felt is 'a feeling' may be one of those deceptive common-sense suppositions inherent in the structure of language which semanticists are constantly bringing to our attention. 'Feeling' is a verbal noun— . . , that psychologically makes an entity out of process. To feel is to do something, not to have something; . . . What is felt is a process, perhaps a large complex of processes, within the organism." Langer, *op. cit.*, pp. 20–21.

69. May, "The Significance of Symbols," in *Symbolism in Religion and Literature, op. cit.*, p. 34.

70. *Ibid.*, p. 45.

71. "Awareness in the ordinary workday paradoxically serves an efficient and sensitizing and yet blinding function. Were this not so, our lives would have little stability. For the most part, conceptual contact with the objects, places and events we encounter takes place at the lowest common denominator of identity." George S. Klein, "Consciousness in Psychoanalytic Theory: Some Implications for Current Research in Perception," in *Contemporary Psychology: Selected*

Essays, ed. Richard M. Jones (New York: Harper & Row, 1967), p. 174.

72. See my "The Christian and the Atheist," in *A Time to Build, op. cit.,* pp. 51–59.
73. I Corinthians 4:5.
74. See Levi-Strauss, *Structural Anthropology,* trans. Claire Jacobson and Brooke Grundfest Schoepf (Garden City, N.Y.: Doubleday & Co., 1967),p. 208; Also see Leonard G. Ratner's *Music: The Listener's Art* (New York: Macmillan Co., 1957).

4. Myths and Institutions

1. Peter L. Berger and Thomas Luckmann, *The Social Construction of Reality: A Treatise in the Sociology of Knowledge* (Garden City, N.Y.: Doubleday & Co., 1966).
2. "Before the sixties, if memory serves, those of us who rejected the dogmatic and the doctrinaire as incompatible with the search for truth were similarly hostile to any apocalyptic view of human experience and history—that is, to any interpretation that led to certain cataclysm or Armageddon. It seemed a form of extremism—it was *de trop,* ahistorical, determinist, neurotic. True, there were nuclear weapons in overabundant supply then, and in the late forties and early fifties, when Stalin governed in Moscow and proponents of 'preventive' or 'pre-emptive' war were now and then to be encountered here, some of us felt constrained to point out that the end could come at any moment unless certain steps were taken—or if certain steps were taken. But the anxieties of those days sprang from no particular view of history; they seemed solidly based on empirical analysis of the available data. . . .

"The mood [of apocalyse] hit me with an almost incapacitating force some six or seven years ago. Or perhaps, since I cannot be precise about the time, it might be better to say that it did not hit me so much as creep over me and produce near-paralysis.

"Up to then, I had gone about my business, as in general I still do, with rather little in the way of metaphysical baggage. Like Mr. Justice Holmes, I traveled more comfortably that way, and I emulated him by limiting my 'truths' to 'what I can't help thinking.' But I now realize that I was sustained throughout—more subconsciously than otherwise, I think—by a kind of social Darwinism, a not very clearly formulated belief that man, though more often than not a player in tragedy, could and would somehow, as William Faulkner (hardly a social Darwinist) had said, 'prevail.'

"I doubt if I ever tried to defend this view, even to myself. Had I done so, I might have discovered that it was probably not so much a 'view' as it was an assumption necessary to my life as a writer of the sort I was and am. One has a need to believe in the future if one is to poke around in the past or in the present. Otherwise, why bother? Why bother?—I must, in the past few years, have spent several thousand man-hours worrying this question before thrusting it aside and attacking the typewriter." Richard H. Rovere, "The Sixties: 'This

Slum of a Decade'," *The New York Times Magazine*, December 4, 1969, pp. 25–26.

3. "A revolted one, a revolutionary, will for a long time affect a kind of reserve: he will not permit the loss of what Harlem has named his 'cool,' . . . To be cool is to float upon one's decisions, to remain positioned just barely beyond the reach of one's commitments. To be cool is to act freedom out without quite denying that there is a hoax involved. . . . He may very well piece together an entire habit of life out of hesitation, ambiguity, reserve. He is oblique, ironic, elegant, and cool, someone whose detachment tries not to become treachery, whose sympathy tries not to become irreversible involvement." Carl Oglesby, "The Revolted," *Containment and Change* (New York: Macmillan Co., Collier Books, 1967), pp. 149–53.

4. Laing, *op. cit.*, pp. 59–60.

5. Sullivan, *op. cit.*, pp. 7–12.

6. "The incompatibility of early childhood experience with the categories and the organization of adult memory is to a large extent due to what I call the conventionalization of the adult memory. . . . Obviously the schemata of experience as well as of memory are determined by the culture which has developed a certain view of the world and of life, a view which furnishes the schemata for all experience and all memory. . . . By conventionalization of the memory (and experience) schemata I understand those memory processes which are . . . not capable of reproducing individual experience, but can only reproduce what John Doe is supposed to have experienced according to the Joneses' and everybody else's ideas of what people experience . . . [the small child] is a little animal, a little heathen, and his experiences are only gradually and increasingly forced into the Procrustean bed of the culturally prevalent experience schemata which allow for certain experiences, forbid others, and omit a great many for which the culture has either no frame of reference or only an unsuitable one." Schachtel, *op. cit.*, pp. 294–95, 97.

7. "The average adult . . . has ceased to wonder, to discover. . . . It is this adult who answers the child's questions and, in answering, fails to answer them but instead acquaints the child with the conventional patterns of his civilization, which effectively close up the asking mouth and shut the wondering eye. Franz Kafka once formulated this aspect of education by saying that 'probably all education is but two things, first, parrying of the ignorant children's impetuous assault on the truth and, second, gentle, imperceptible, step-by-step initiation of the humiliated children into the lie.' " *Ibid.*, pp. 292–93.

8. See David Riesman, et. al., *The Lonely Crowd* (Garden City, N.Y.: Doubleday & Co., 1953), pp. 34–48.

9. "The decaying structure of American 'holidays' as occasions continually rebuilding common sentiment is a mute and too little recognized evidence of this process of emotional disintegration. Washington's Birthday, Lincoln's Birthday, Decoration Day, the Fourth of July, and Labor Day have lost their ceremonial observations and are occasions for private holiday; while Thanksgiving is so sunk in football games and turkey-dinners that the annual Presidential procla-

mation has become a quaint curiosity . . . they formerly helped to contribute the binding mortar of common sentiment to the culture; and as their specific traditional meanings have worn thin to modern man, they have simply been abandoned and no emotionally rich substitutes put in their place." Robert S. Lynd, *Knowledge for What?* (New York: Grove Press, 1964), p. 84; see also pp. 80–87.

10. See Harvey Cox, *The Secular City: A Celebration of its Liberties and an Invitation to its Disciplines* (New York: Macmillan Co., 1965).

11. May, "The Significance of Symbols," *Symbolism in Religion and Literature, op. cit.*, p. 24.

12. *Ibid.*, p, 23.

13. *Ibid.*, p. 28.

14. *Ibid.*, p. 23.

15. *Ibid.*, pp. 23–24.

16. *Ibid.*, pp. 28–29.

17. ". . . The kind of logic in mythical thought is as rigorous as that of modern science, and . . . the difference lies, not in the quality of the intellectual process, but in the nature of the things to which it is applied." Levi-Strauss, *Structural Anthropology, op. cit.*, p. 227; "Certainly the properties to which the savage mind has access are not the same as those which have commanded the attention of scientists. The physical world is approached from opposite ends in the two cases: one is supremely concrete, the other supremely abstract; one proceeds from the angle of sensible quanlities and the other from that of formal properties." Levi-Strauss, *The Savage Mind* (Chicago: University of Chicago Press, 1966), p. 269; See his *Totemism, op. cit.*, p. 96; see also Geoffrey Hartman, "Structuralism: The Anglo-American Adventure," *Yale French Studies*, 36–37 (1966): 154.

18. Heisenberg, op. cit., p. 227.

19. *Ibid.*, pp. 223–24.

20. *Ibid.*, p. 224; Lewis Mumford questioned this connection between science and technology, and demanded that "science release itself from the humanly impoverished and under-dimensioned mythology of power that Francis Bacon helped to promote." In Gerald Holton, *Science and Culture* (Boston: Beacon Press, 1967), p. xxii, n. 12.

21. *Time*, January 3, 1969, p. 17.

22. *Ibid.*

23. Lasswell, *Politics, op. cit.*, pp. 177–78.

24. "What . . . is your Fourth of July? . . . To [the black man] your celebration is a sham; your boasted liberty, an unholy licence; your national greatness, welling vanity; your sounds of rejoicing are empty and heartless; your denunciation of tyrants, brass-fronted impudence; your shouts of liberty and equality, hollow mockery; your prayers and hymns, your sermons and thanksgivings, with all your religious parade and solemnity, are, to him, mere bombast, fraud, deception, impiety and hypocrisy—a thin veil to cover up crimes which would disgrace a nation of savages." (Frederick Douglass, 1852).

After quoting this, Cleaver comments: "For all these years whites have been taught to believe in the myth they preached, while Negroes have had to face the bitter reality of what America practiced." *Op. cit.*, pp. 75, 77.

25. May, *op. cit.*, pp. 11–12; the article by Whitehead is "Uses of Symbolism." Whitehead does not himself wish to "push aside symbols," arguing instead that mankind needs to express himself in symbols but that these need continual revision. *Ibid.*, pp. 233–50.

26. "One result of the externalizing of fantasy in our civilization has been discipline in the special pattern of thinking which we call analytical. The play of fantasy has been continually subordinated to the material world. The goal of fantasy has steadily become the forecasting of sequences in the material environment. The role of hypothesis is to prefigure reality, and speculative fantasy turns again and again to symbols which stand for routines in externality. . . . The prestige of the analytical pattern of thought is due to the receptivities which have been developed for any expedient which could furnish 'leads' for the discovery of routines in nature which might be presently utilized in partially remodeling the environment." Lasswell, *World Politics, op. cit.*, p. 205.

27. Jerome S. Bruner, "The Course of Cognitive Growth," *Contemporary Educational Psychology: Selected Essays, op. cit.*, pp. 124–25.

28. *Ibid.*, p. 153.

29. Jones, op. cit., pp. 123–24.

30. Jerry Farber, "The Student as Nigger," (Los Angeles: Los Angeles Free Press, Underground Press Syndicate, n.d.).

31. John W. M. Whiting and Irvin L. Child, *Child Training and Personality* (New Haven: Yale University Press, 1967), pp. 91–94.

32. The proclivity of the analytic mind for images of hardness can scarcely be overlooked: hardnosed, hardheaded, hard facts. Is it related to the yearning of intellectuals in a business culture to assert their masculinity? See Richard Hofstadter, *Anti-Intellectualism in American Life* (New York: Random House, Vintage Books, 1966) pp. 188–96, 226–29, 320; Christopher Lasch, *The New Radicalism in America (1889–1963): The Intellectual as a Social Type* (New York: Alfred A. Knopf, 1965), pp. 308–12ff.

33. Lasswell, *Politics op. cit.*, p. 202.

34. *Ibid.*, p. 42.

35. *Ibid.*, p. 31.

36. *Ibid.*, p. 32.

37. *Ibid.*

38. *Ibid.*, p. 33.

39. *Ibid.*

40. *Ibid.*, pp. 33–34.

41. *Ibid.*, p. 34.

42. "The rebellion of the oppressed peoples of the world, along with the Negro revolution in America, have opened the way to a new evaluation of history, a re-examination of the role played by the white race since the beginning of European expansion. . . . Slave-catchers, slaveowners, murderers, butchers, invaders, oppressors—the white heroes have acquired new names. The great white statesmen whom school children are taught to revere are revealed as the

architects of systems of human exploitation and slavery. Religious leaders are exposed as condoners and justifiers of all these evil deeds. Schoolteachers and college professors are seen as a clique of brainwashers and whitewashers.

"The white youth of today are coming to see, intuitively, that to escape the onus of the history their fathers made they must face and admit the moral truth concerning the works of their fathers. That such venerated figures as George Washington and Thomas Jefferson owned hundreds of black slaves, that all of the Presidents up to Lincoln presided over a slave state, and that every president since Lincoln connived politically and cynically with the issues affecting the human rights and general welfare of the broad masses of the American people —these facts weigh heavily upon the hearts of these young people. . . . The foundations of authority have been blasted to bits in America because the whole society has been indicted, tried, and convicted of injustice. To the youth, the elders are Ugly Americans; to the elders, the youth have gone mad." Cleaver, *op. cit.*, pp. 70–71.

43. Lasswell, *Politics, op. cit.*, p. 31.
44. "The community guardians ('We') symbolize the conscience of the community: . . . A college president, a bishop, an army general, is expected to relate action to the 'sacred principles' of learning, religion, or defense, not to question such principles, to offer original views about them, or to open institutional ends, values, and purposes to doubt and inquiry." Hugh Dalziel Duncan, *Symbols in Society* (New York: Oxford University Press, 1968), pp. 95–96; see also pp. 52, 116–18.
45. Social systems are enacted as social dramas, and their actors play roles which are firmly established by tradition; elites which deviate from their assigned roles risk losing authority. "Beliefs in authority are not abstractions, but dramatic rules of conduct." *Ibid.*, p. 204.
46. Edelman, *op. cit.*
47. *Ibid.*, pp. 2–3, 27–28, 122–23.
48. "Thus administrative decision-makers on the regulatory commissions function in a setting in which they become in effect part of the management of the industry they are to regulate. They are forcefully and regularly bombarded with statements of the various costs confronting the industry and with its business problems; they associate formally and often informally with its top officers, learning their perspectives and their values. At the same time they are kept intensely aware of the sanctions that await them and the agency if these business and organizational considerations are ignored: congressional displeasure, public attacks, probable displacement at the end of their terms of office. Even more obviously, their careers and prestige are now tied to the industry. As the industry grows, so does their function and importance; if the industry dies, so does the agency. Symbiosis ripens into osmosis and digestion. There is no significant difference between this situation and that of the corporation officers themselves.

"The organizational and psychological embrace of the industry around the regulatory commissioners go hand in hand. To be part of the organization in the sense of incessant exposure to its problems and decisional premises is to come to share its perspectives and values. This is not 'pressure'; it is absorption." *Ibid.*, p. 66; see also pp. 38 42, 52, 54–55, 63–67.

49. "The chief executive may maintain his 'symbolic leadership' through ascriptions of his ability to cope, through publicized action on noncontroversial policies or on trivia, and through a dramaturgical performance emphasizing the traits popularly associated with leadership: forcefulness, responsibility, courage, decency, and so on.

"Thus, . . . survey research [indicates] that 'Eisenhower's lack of commitments at [that] time simply encouraged his supporters to see him either as a non-partisan national leader, or as an unspoken sympathizer with their own views.' . . . In an ambiguous situation people may, as the result of their own anxieties, perceive a leader's acts to be what they want them to be." *Ibid.*, p. 81; see also pp. 78–94; on symbolic reassurance, see pp. 9, 12–13, 22, 32, 38, 40, 41–43, 170–71, 188–94.

50. *Ibid.*, pp. 44–50, 158–59.
51. *Ibid.*, p. 150.
52. *Ibid.*, p. 45.
53. "Observation of politics is not simply an effort to learn what is happening but rather a process of making observations conform to assumptions.

"The student of political process therefore makes a serious mistake if he takes political perceptions and verbal justifications of political attitudes as fixed entities that predict future behavior and attitudes. They will do so only as long as the respondents continue to respond to the same symbols through taking the same roles. Perception of political events and rationalizations of political attitudes are to be understood not as independent variables or as causes of behavior, but rather as signals of a particular kind of role taking and symbolization. Only when they are studied as such signals do they become clues to political dynamics.

"Only then, for example, does it become clear that a succession of conspicuous events in the news is routinely perceived by a group as having particular metaphorical meaning, no matter what the events may be, while the same series of events may have a quite different meaning for a group reacting to different symbols. For one group a Khruschev ultimatum on Berlin is a necessary reaction to American war mongering and his later withdrawal of the ultimatum is confirmation of his ambition for peace. To another group the ultimatum 'proves' the assumption that Khruschev is intent on creating a casus belli, while his withdrawal is perceived as a tactical ploy, evidence of his shiftiness and aggressive intent." *Ibid.*, p. 186.

54. *Ibid.*, pp. 158–59, 60, 134–38, 145–49.
55. *Ibid.*, pp. 121, 124–27.
56. Tillich, "The Religious Symbol," in *Symbolism in Religion and Literature, op. cit.*, p. 88n.
57. Camus, *The Myth of Sisyphus, op. cit.*, p. 88–91.
58. Hannah Arendt notes that the decisive experience of young people today is that of a technology which is not like earlier forms of technology but "seems in so

many instances to lead straight into disaster" and "far from threatening only certain classes with unemployment, menaces the very existence of whole nations and conceivably of all mankind." See her "Reflections on Violence," *Journal of International Affairs* 23, no. 1 (1969): 7. See, especially, her note 14: "Nathan Glazer, in an article on 'Student Power at Berkeley' in *The Public Interest*'s interesting Special Issue *The Universities*, Fall 1968, writes: 'The student radicals . . . remind me more of the Luddite machines smashers than the Socialist trade unionists who achieved citizenship and power for workers,' and he concludes from this impression that Zbigniew Brzezinski (in an article about Columbia in *The New Republic*, June 1, 1968) may have been right in his diagnosis: 'Very frequently revolutions are the last spasm of the past, and thus are not really revolutions but counter-revolutions, operating in the name of revolutions.' Isn't this bias in favor of marching forward at any price rather odd in two authors who are generally considered to be conservatives? And isn't it even more odd that Glazer should remain unaware of the decisive differences between manufacturing machinery in early nineteenth-century England and the hardware developed in the middle of the twentieth century much of which is for destruction and can't even be smashed by the rebels for the simple reason that they know neither where it is located nor how to smash it."

The Bross Foundation

The Bross Foundation

In 1879, William Bross of Chicago established at Lake Forest College the Bross Foundation, the income from the fund to be used to stimulate the production of the best books or treatises "on the connection, relation and mutual bearing on any practical science, or the history of our race, or the facts in any department of knowledge, with and upon the Christian Religion." From time to time until his death in 1890, Mr. Bross made contributions to the fund, which was to serve as a memorial to his son, Nathaniel, who died in 1856.

To achieve his aim, Mr. Bross provided that competitions should be conducted every decade, the winning manuscript to be published by the Foundation. He also asked that the Trustees of the Bross Foundation purchase suitable manuscripts which it would then publish. This volume, the 18th in the Bross Library, is in the latter category. The next competition closes in September, 1970.

Other volumes in the Bross Library include the first one, *Evidences of Christianity* by Mark Hopkins, published in 1880, *The Sources of Religious Insight* by Josiah Royce in 1911, *Modern Poetry and the Christian Tradition* by Amos N. Wilder in 1952 and *Language and Faith: Studies in Sign, Symbol and Meaning* by John A. Hutchison, the 17th volume, published in 1963.

147

72 73 10 9 8 7 6 5 4